Teaching Mathematics through Story

'It is enormously important to engage young children in maths so that the foundations are understood and enjoyed. The outcomes of such engagement are long lasting in their benefits for later learning. This book illustrates the role that storytelling can play in mastering the fundamental skills of maths, such as problem solving and number sense. The book is written and illustrated in a persuasive and engaging way and offers a vital insight into early maths education.'

Steve Chinn, independent international lecturer,
writer and researcher, and author of *The Trouble
with Maths*, now in its second edition

How do you make mathematics relevant and exciting to young children? How can mathematics and literacy be combined in a meaningful way? How can stories inspire the teaching and learning of mathematics?

This book explores the exciting ways in which story can be used as a flexible resource to facilitate children's mathematical thinking. It looks at the potential relationship between story and mathematics and practically demonstrates how they can be combined to help children connect, understand and express mathematical ideas using story language.

Written for all early years practitioners and students, the book offers a playful pedagogical approach to facilitating children's mathematical thinking, which brings a creative satisfaction and confidence to teaching mathematics. Encouraging a creative approach to teaching mathematics that draws on picture books and oral mathematical stories, the book shows you how to:

- move from reading to telling stories with mathematical themes;
- encourage children to pose and solve problems by playing with the plot of stories;
- enable children to translate abstract mathematical ideas to concrete representations with supporting story props and puppets;
- create original oral mathematical stories alongside children;
- capture children's mathematical thinking in an observational framework, supported with audio or video recordings that can be shared with parents and colleagues.

There are free audio recordings of children and adults telling oral mathematical stories that feature in the book. These can be downloaded from: www.routledge.com/9780415688154.

This book draws on practical work with children, educators, parents, professional storytellers and trainee practitioners, who bring theoretical ideas to life and offer insight into their mathematical story experiences. It is a 'must have' for all those who want to make mathematics relevant, accessible and imaginative for young children.

Caroline McGrath is a lecturer for the Early Childhood Studies Foundation Degree, in partnership with Plymouth University, at City of Bristol College. She has a particular interest in children's mathematical development, and is the author of *Supporting Early Mathematical Development: Practical approaches to play-based learning* (Routledge, 2010). Her research involving children, educators and staff informs the content of this new book.

Teaching Mathematics through Story

A creative approach for the early years

Caroline McGrath

Routledge
Taylor & Francis Group

LONDON AND NEW YORK

First published 2014
by Routledge
2 Park Square, Milton Park, Abingdon, Oxon OX14 4RN

and by Routledge
711 Third Avenue, New York, NY 10017

Routledge is an imprint of the Taylor & Francis Group, an informa business

British Library Cataloguing in Publication Data
A catalogue record for this book is available from the British Library

Library of Congress Cataloging in Publication Data
McGrath, Caroline.
   Teaching mathematics through story: a creative approach for the early
   years/Caroline McGrath.
   pages cm
   1. Arithmetic – Study and teaching (Elementary).   2. Mathematics –
   Study and teaching (Elementary).   3. Storytelling in education.
   4. Effective teaching.   I. Title.
   QA107.2.M43 2014
   372.7 – dc23
   2013050808

ISBN: 978-0-415-68814-7 (hbk)
ISBN: 978-0-415-68815-4 (pbk)
ISBN: 978-0-203-35739-2 (ebk)

Typeset in Helvetica Neue
by Florence Production Ltd, Stoodleigh, Devon, UK

Printed and bound in Great Britain by
TJ International Ltd, Padstow, Cornwall

Contents

List of figures   vii
Acknowledgements   ix

Introduction   1

1 **Mathematics**   5

2 **Story**   20

3 **Threading play in a mathematical way**   33

4 **Picture books: meaningful mathematical contexts**   45

5 **Oral mathematical story: moving from picture books to oral mathematical story**   57

6 **Oral mathematical story: possibilities**   70

7 **Oral mathematical story: large and small groups**   83

8 **Puppets and props: mathematical stories in their making**   97

9 **Children as mathematical storytellers**   112

10 **Crafting and telling oral mathematical stories**   126

Conclusion   138

Appendix 1 Mathematical observation tool   144
Appendix 2 Story profile template   146

v

Contents

Appendix 3 Story profile: 'Handa's Surprise' by Eileen Browne   148
Appendix 4 Story profile: 'The Doorbell Rang' by Pat Hutchins   150
Appendix 5 Story profile: 'Little Lumpty' by Miko Imai   152
Appendix 6 How to make a gorilla hand puppet   154

References   157
Bibliography   162
Index   165

Figures

1.1 Aeroplane! (Browne & Parkins 1993)   6
1.2 Shrew follows instructions and sets out parts to make the aeroplane (Browne & Parkins 1993)   8–9
1.3 An observational tool to capture children's mathematical behaviour based on the format for Learning Stories (Carr 2001)   17
1.4 Jake retelling 'Ladybird on a Leaf' using a sugar paper ladybird and spots   18
2.1 A monkey takes a banana from Handa's basket of seven fruits (Browne 1998)   21
2.2 Ikran playfully dramatises 'Handa's Surprise'   31
3.1 Jake playing with 'Ladybird on a Leaf' story-related props to create the pattern $12 - n + n = 12$ 40
3.2 Completed observational tool   42–43
4.1 A child using Polydron to make a box for a cat after listening to the story 'My Cat Likes to Hide in Boxes'   49
5.1 Little Lumpty (story prop to support telling of adapted oral version)   58
5.2 Little Lumpty climbs the wall and the gap between the rungs of his ladder is equivalent to two bricks   63
6.1 Children draw on clipboards while listening to an oral mathematical story (legitimate peripheral participants)   78
6.2 Nesta's clipboard drawing (five years and two months) represents ten spots and eight spots on a ladybird after listening to a version of 'Ladybird on a Leaf' where the mathematical ideas $5 + 5 - 5 = 5$ and $5 + 3 - 3 = 5$ are expressed   78
6.3 Children engaging as part of a retelling of 'The Enormous Turnip' with Kirsty Burns   81
7.1 Louise Cheshire (Reception class teacher) retelling 'The Greedy Triangle'   85
7.2 Suzanne (Reception class teacher) relaxed and confident as a storyteller   86

7.3	Suzanne (Reception class teacher) sitting 'alongside' children as a story listener	87
8.1	Props made by Rebecca Belsten for 'The Elves and the Shoemaker'	98
8.2	Children enjoying the story props and 'not one, not two but three elves' seeing even and odd numbers	101
8.3	Rachel Adcock introducing 'Goodnight Gorilla' using the gorilla hand puppet she made	103
8.4	Daniel retells 'Ladybird on a Leaf' using the prop as a story character and the spots as concrete representations of his mathematical ideas	106
8.5	A child looking at Little Lumpty's design	107
8.6	Children holding Rebecca's shoemaker props and asking how they were made	108
8.7	Rebecca sharing her prop making guide with a child	109
9.1	Fish patterns on the carpet as part of children retelling 'Penguin'	114
9.2	Freya using fish to tell 'Penguin'	116
9.3	Mya holds Little Lumpty ready to tell a story, which involves him counting in multiples of five to steady his nerves as he climbs a ladder	122
9.4	Anna using Little Lumpty at the start of the count	123
10.1	Kirsty Burns sets up a room with props for telling 'The Enormous Turnip' with Reception class children	129
10.2	Mya writes out her mathematical idea for Little Lumpty 'counting in multiples of fives'	131
C.1	Collection of six cushions inviting small group oral mathematical storytelling	138

Acknowledgements

I am grateful to the children, staff and parents of children and students of early years practice who have contributed to the research project that informs this book. These particularly include the children and staff at Ashley Down Infants School, Bristol. Susie Weaver, who was acting head teacher at Ashley Down Infants School at the outset of the project (now head of Wallscourt Farm Academy, Bristol), facilitated the research project and contributed to discussions that led to the development of ideas. In particular I thank Lucy Walshe, Louise Cheshire, Suzanne Kelham and Kirsty Burns, who actively participated and were willing to try a different approach alongside daily commitments that whole class teaching brings. I also wish to acknowledge the encouragement given by all staff at the school and parents who willingly gave permission for their children to be video and audio recorded. Contributions from Anna Welsh, Heather Nicol, Dawn Balogun-Adeola, Jean Maggs, Claire Williams, David Branfield, Charlie Baughan and Jane Robinson as educationalists are acknowledged. I also acknowledge my daughter Orna, who provided very early home-based ideas that opened out possibilities that could be tested before taking them to other settings.

My thanks are also due to Dr Julia Morgan and Dr Nicholas Pratt for their inspiration and support. Discussions at Plymouth University helped to shape some of the ideas and to develop a theoretical perspective.

I thank two professional storytellers whom I admire: Cassandra Wye and Paula Brown. Cassandra contributes to the training of early years practitioners and educationalists worldwide. Paula works more locally in the Bristol area. I thank Veronika Frydrychová, who made the story props, for example Little Lumpty, which captivate children. I thank students who surprise me and in particular Rebecca Belsten and Rachel Adcock, who contributed willingly to this work and brought much joy to children who heard their oral mathematical stories and played with their puppet and props. I thank Douglas Hook who took some of the photographs with sensitivity and professionalism.

I would like to thank Frances Shillaber, who in her capacity as Local Education Authority Advisor offered invaluable advice and guidance. I also express thanks to Olaf Raetzel for offering guidance and for thoughtful suggestions on development of ideas. Authors of children's literature such as Eileen Browne deserve much in the way of recognition and I value their contribution.

Stephen Atkinson deserves a special mention for his ongoing support and encouragement with projects that span many years. Without these people mentioned the project would not have developed in the way it did. I am indebted to those that helped and responded with enthusiasm to the idea of trying a different approach.

Introduction

'The Tyger' (1794)

Tyger! Tyger, burning bright
In the forests of the night,
What immortal hand or eye
Could frame thy fearful symmetry?

Blake (1905)

Augustus the tiger was sad because he lost his smile (Rayner 2008). Augustus searches bushes, trees, mountains, oceans, deserts, puddles, before realising his smile is there whenever he is happy. Blake searches for a force beyond man to capture the power of his 'Tyger'. The children's story and the adult poem each feature a tiger and bring mathematical possibilities, should we look for them.

William Blake's poem is about the work of man and the work of nature. Mathematics encompasses nature, history, literature and philosophy and 'flowers as part of human culture' (Hersh 1998, p.218). Augustus stalks through a sequence of places on a journey: there is a pattern to the language of his story, there is a problem posed and a solution found; there is symmetry to his story.

We engage our imagination and emotions as we follow Augustus. Though the loss of a smile is an abstract idea, there is a simplicity and mystery that we can relate to. The essence of the story can be generalised to us as individuals.

A story can place mathematical ideas intentionally or unintentionally into a meaningful context. Story has been used to explain difficult concepts such as gravity and relativity. Davies (2007) describes how storytelling can be used across the curriculum to break down subjects that are difficult to learn and how they can be made accessible.

The mathematical possibilities within a story are often plentiful even when they are unintended or unplanned by the author (Browne 2013; Burroway 2009). Undiscovered opportunities to teach mathematics through story emerge repeatedly. Children may relate to the character of Augustus: the emotion evoked through the problem of losing something precious; the satisfaction of finding what was lost. There is the possibility of playing with this plot: what if Augustus never finds his smile, realises tigers never smile or meets a leopard on the way? Blake asks a metaphysical and metaphorical question: 'What immortal hand or eye, could frame thy fearful symmetry?', though symmetry in nature never truly exists. Pound and Lee point out the difficulties adults and children have identifying characteristics of pattern and explain that '[z]ebra skin, for example, is not regular or symmetrical but it is a pattern because it is identifiable as such' (2011, p.129). Children and adults can pose problems in a similar way to Blake in his poem and, in doing so, engage in mathematical thinking.

This book has three aims: to explore story as a pedagogical tool to teach mathematics, to find out what happens when this approach is taken and to encourage children and adults to work with oral mathematical story. The book is informed by a project that contributes to research about the potential to facilitate children's mathematical thinking through story for children aged between four and seven.

Much of the available literature looks at how story can be used to teach literacy, but this book looks specifically at using story and oral story to teach mathematics to young children. Readers will explore the 'tremendous versatility of story as a pedagogic tool' (Grugeon & Gardner 2000, p.58) with a particular emphasis on the teaching of mathematics.

The word 'adult' throughout this book includes teachers, educators, teaching assistants, early years practitioners, students, parents and all others concerned with the education of young children. It is intended that theoretical material in the text along with practical ideas and tools can be used in ways that suit individual readers. Earlier chapters are more theoretical in content, setting out a foundation on which the more practical work is structured. These earlier chapters include theoretical perspectives that lead to devising practical tools: a mathematical observation format based on Learning Stories for assessment (Carr 2001); a story profile for the analysis of and creation of stories; a supportive-learning characteristics framework for selecting and analysis of picture books. The book can be read in a flexible way, with some readers preferring to follow the journey from start to end and others deciding to start at different places, returning to earlier chapters later. Certain points echo through chapters because they relate to different contexts and allow for flexibility in reading the text. Copies of materials to support work in practice are included in the Appendices.

The use of story as a resource adds another dimension to teaching mathematics. The reader is encouraged to explore skills including dismantling story to uncover mathematical opportunity, making mathematical connections through story and rebuilding and creating original mathematical story. Practical approaches are considered with exemplar stories from practitioners and published sources. As adults it can be difficult to be creative and yet we expect this of children. The book presents techniques to help us take on the challenges of being creative mathematical educators.

This book draws on work with children, professional storytellers, early years teachers, teaching assistants and students of an Early Childhood Studies foundation degree. The work offers alternative approaches that complement existing pedagogical choices for mathematics. Throughout the text I draw on my experience as a qualified teacher and lecturer for an Early Childhood Studies foundation degree. The writing of this book coincides with PhD research. I observe children responding to oral story and, with a keen researcher's eye, examine children's play and story retellings through a mathematical lens. I take the role of oral storyteller and invite teachers to observe how children respond to stories.

As part of this creative approach there are a number of relationships to work with, including relationships between stories read and stories told, mathematics and story, mathematics and play. The spontaneous talk of children playing and retelling mathematical stories is recounted with a view to gaining insights into children's mathematical thinking.

Stories are analysed and these profiles provide a sense of what the mathematical possibilities are and how story can be played with to prompt mathematical thinking. Mathematical ideas can be mapped out in advance, which gives the oral mathematical storyteller insights that could otherwise be missed. Examples of problem posing, problem solving, patterning, counting, adding, subtracting, multiplying and dividing are considered. This book uses picture books, traditional stories and oral story as resources to engage children mathematically. While stories in books can be used to support children's mathematical development, this text will illustrate the role of oral story in taking this further. This includes consideration of the scope for playing with story plot to prompt mathematical thinking.

Chapter 1 offers a theoretical perspective about some of the features of mathematics. There is a particular focus on problem posing and problem solving and later these ideas serve to offer insight into children posing and solving problems in play and as storytellers. An observational tool to capture children's mathematical behaviour in play and as storytellers is presented. This tool allows the observer to see children's play and storytelling in a mathematical way.

Chapter 2 gives a theoretical perspective about story. Terms are defined so that shared understanding is established, and techniques that influence the pattern of story are explored. The components and qualities of story are highlighted and offered as a story profile. This story profile can be used to guide creation of original stories with mathematical possibilities.

Chapter 3 offers a theoretical perspective on play, identifying play as both implicitly and explicitly mathematical. The chapter describes children expressing explicit mathematical ideas in play and considers children as mathematical narrative authors in play.

Chapter 4 promotes the idea of children's literature as a pedagogical choice to support mathematics. The chapter identifies supportive learning characteristics of picture books. There is a detailed analysis of 'The Doorbell Rang' by Pat Hutchins (1986) with a practical application of the supportive-learning characteristics proposed by Van den Heuvel-Panhuizen and Elia (2012).

Chapters 5, 6 and 7 are a cluster of chapters about oral mathematical story experiences. Chapter 5 is about moving from reading a book with mathematical possibility to telling the story without a book. Chapter 6 focuses on the scope of possibilities, including creative dialogue, which oral mathematical story brings. The challenges of telling oral mathematical story to large groups are documented based on the experiences of teachers and storytellers who take this approach. Chapter 7 opens out oral mathematical story to smaller groups. In these smaller groups the adult is 'alongside' the children (Haynes & Murris 2012). The chapter describes ways in which some children respond to small group oral mathematical storytelling and make mathematical connections.

Chapter 8 considers how puppets and props connect story, mathematics, storyteller and listener in purposeful ways. Puppets and props can be used to make mathematical ideas explicit, which is necessary for young children. This chapter provides accounts of how trainee early years practitioners make props and puppets. Students' reflective accounts tell the stories of creating 'Gorilla', a hand puppet, and props for 'The Elves and the Shoemaker'.

Chapter 9 concerns how children retell oral mathematical stories in remarkable ways. An audio recording of Freya retelling an oral mathematical story is transcribed, and descriptions of children serve to show how the use of oral narrative story in learning environments promotes mathematical thinking in children.

Chapter 10 covers guidance on the crafting and telling of oral mathematical story. There are practical suggestions on how to optimise this creative opportunity.

This book is intended to support student teachers, educationalists and other adults interested in facilitating children's creative mathematical thinking. The creative pedagogical choice described is proposed as an alternative that complements other approaches to teaching mathematics (Schiro 2004; Pound & Lee 2011). The content of this book poses and offers some response to the following questions:

- What are the mathematical opportunities in picture books?
- How can we move from sharing a picture book to telling an adapted version of this story orally?
- How do children respond to oral mathematical story?
- What are the challenges around the use of oral story to facilitate children's mathematical thinking?

In summary, this book is about the potential of using the relationship between mathematics and story with young children. The reader is taken through a series of progressive stages, which enable dismantling, rebuilding and creating mathematical story. The possibility of promoting mathematical thinking through story is at the heart of each chapter.

Most people may be unsure of their ability to create any story, never mind a mathematical story. Telling stories is an art that we can acquire, practice and polish (Grugeon & Gardner 2000). I present insights and skills that result in a creative pedagogic tool to support teaching of mathematics through story. I hope you enjoy teaching mathematics through story; being the educationalist who finds their smile.

◀))) *There are free audio recordings of children and adults telling oral mathematical stories that feature in the book. These can be downloaded from:* www.routledge.com/9780415688154.

Mathematics

Mathematics unfolds, like a flower opening, or a tree plunging roots deeper and crown higher.

(Hersh 1998, p.86)

This chapter aims to explore:

- problem posing and problem solving
- making mathematical generalisations
- an observational tool to conceptualise mathematics and capture children's mathematical behaviour in play and as storytellers.

'No Problem!'

'One morning, Mouse was woken up by a heavy CLONK! outside her front door. Whatever's that? Mouse thought. She nipped out of bed, opened the door and looked outside. In front of her was an ENORMOUS parcel. It was wrapped in brown paper and tied with string.

CONSTRUCTION KIT was stamped on the front and a pink card hung from the side. It read:

To Mouse,
Put together the things you see,
Then climb aboard and visit me!
Love from Rat.

"Oooooh!" squeaked Mouse.
She nibbled through the string, peeled off the paper and opened the parcel.
Inside was a mountain of bits and pieces – just *waiting* to be put together.
Mouse sniffed them and snuffled them.
She poked them and prodded them.
"I can put these together," she said.
"NO problem."

She was in such a hurry to begin that she forgot to look for the instructions.
She didn't see the sheet of paper that said:

CONSTRUCTION KIT. HOW TO PUT IT TOGETHER!

Mouse set to work.
She joined pipes here and fixed wheels there.
She twisted and turned things.
She fiddled and twiddled things.
She bolted bolts and tightened nuts.'

Mouse makes something that looks like a bike but isn't a bike. She calls it a 'Bikeoodle-Doodle' but didn't get far before meeting Badger. Badger asks if there are any instructions and offers to fix it. Badger makes what looks like a car and calls it a 'Jaloppy-Doppy', which doesn't work. Mouse and Badger meet Otter, who also asks if they have the instructions before offering to help and makes what looks like a boat; he calls it 'a Boater-Roater', which doesn't work terribly well. They meet Shrew who finds the instructions, sets out all the pieces, follows the instructions and makes an aeroplane! They arrive at Rat's house, who asks Mouse if she had any trouble putting the construction kit together: 'No problem' they say!

(Browne & Parkins 1993)

AEROPLANE!

Figure 1.1 Aeroplane! (Browne & Parkins 1993). Text © 1993 Eileen Browne. Illustrations © David Parkins. From 'No Problem!' by Eileen Browne, illustrated by David Parkins. Reproduced by permission of Walker Books Ltd, London SE11 5HJ, www.walker.co.uk

Introduction

The development of mathematical understanding involves building up *connections* in the mind of the child. Our aim is to help children make mathematical connections and build them into a coherent network (Haylock & Cockburn 2013; Suggate *et al.* 2010; 2006). Before exploring how story helps children to make mathematical connections, a variety of ideas about mathematics are explored.

Mathematics is difficult to conceptualise (Casey 2011; 1999) and a tool for observing children's mathematical behaviour is shared to assist with seeing children's play in a mathematical way. This tool can be used to record children, while listening to stories that have mathematical intentions, playing in a mathematical way or retelling mathematical stories. This observational tool is intended to document children's mathematical behaviour in a way that can be readily interpreted, reflected on and shared with other adults and families of children observed (Carr 2001). The observational tool brings theoretical ideas about mathematics and children's practical application of mathematics together and could be complemented with audio recordings of children at play or retelling mathematical stories. I suggest audio as this is less problematic than video in terms of ethical considerations, particularly for those not employed at the setting.

This observational tool is based on a mathematical perspective of Casey (2011; 1999) and principles concerning assessment that led Carr (2001) to the creation of the learning story format for assessment of learning. The intention is that the reader has a way of documenting children's mathematical behaviour in play and as storytellers.

Problem posing and problem solving

We start with a story titled 'No Problem!' by Browne and Parkins (1993). 'No Problem!' reveals several trial and error attempts and a systematic strategy for problem solving: Mouse makes a 'Bikeoodle-Doodle'; Badger makes a 'Jaloppy-Doppy'; Otter makes a 'Boater-Roater'; then we see the required systematic approach for solving this problem as Shrew follows instructions to make an aeroplane. Haylock and Cockburn describe how '[s]olving a problem may be a somewhat chaotic, backwards and forwards, roundabout, hit-and-miss, trial-and-error process, but presenting the solution requires the problem solver to organise his or her ideas into a coherent logical sequence' (2013, p.302). As storytellers we model organising of ideas into a logical sequence when we tell a story.

Problem solving strategies

'No Problem!' expresses at least two different problem solving strategies: trial and error, and systematic thinking; both valuable mathematical strategies to solve problems. Strategies of trial and error produce results but a more systematic approach is required to solve the problem of constructing an aeroplane (Figure 1.2). Haylock and Cockburn (2013) encourage systematic ways of setting out information as this helps children to realise patterns. In order to take flight our stories need to be constructed in a sequential order.

Problem posing and solving connects story and mathematics

Problem posing and problem solving is central to both mathematics and story. Story characters are usually posed with problems that need to be solved. Often a story will have a mathematical idea in there somewhere. Relationships between story and mathematics can be problematised by changing something about the story or about the mathematics: what if Mouse, Badger and Otter do not meet Shrew? What if Shrew has not seen the instructions? A question such as 'what if?' poses a new problem, prompting story and mathematical thinking in order to find new solutions.

Figure 1.2 Shrew follows instructions and sets out parts to make the aeroplane (Browne & Parkins 1993).

Suggesting changes to a story plot potentially poses problems that require mathematical thinking: what if in the story about 'Goldilocks and the Three Bears' Goldilocks goes to the bears' home with a friend? Or it is a family of four bears rather than three? By changing the idea of the story, we create new mathematical problems to think about: how will three bowls of porridge work with two imposters or four bowls of porridge with one?

Problem posing; problem solving; problem creating

The future mathematician should be a clever problem-solver:
but to be a clever problem-solver is not enough.

Polya (1945, p.205)

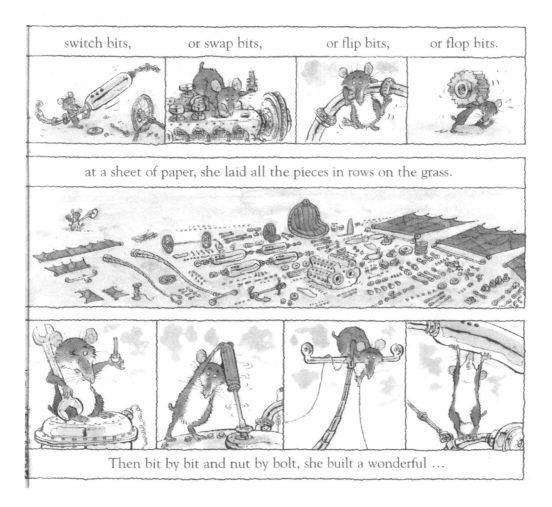

switch bits, or swap bits, or flip bits, or flop bits.

at a sheet of paper, she laid all the pieces in rows on the grass.

Then bit by bit and nut by bolt, she built a wonderful …

Problem posing and solving are required when creating stories: a story is about a problem that needs to be solved. Creating a story requires thinking on a different level to that of retelling a familiar story. Children's creation of stories is evident in play narratives, which we turn to in Chapter 3, and as storytellers, which we come to in Chapter 9.

Companions but different: the relationship between problem posing and problem solving

Mathematics is difficult to define. Hersh (1998, p.18) suggests that questions drive mathematics, and that 'solving problems and making up new ones is the essence of mathematical life'. He describes how 'mathematics is a vast network of interconnected problems and solutions' (Hersh 1998, p.6). The subject is built up by individuals making connections and linking old ideas with new: 'Mathematics is intensely interconnected and self-interactive. The new is vitally linked to the old. The old is revitalised, enriched, and complexified by interaction with the new' (Hersh 1998, p.83). Mathematics is about problem posing, problem solving and making connections between ideas. Having identified problem posing and problem solving as being central to mathematics, we now consider how both differ but make necessary companions.

Problem posing

Among other things, problem posing pursues a particular thread of thinking: 'What if we change something?' Such a question opens a door to problem posing and extension of knowledge (McGrath, 2010). Children may well pose problems without conscious expression through words; adults can think of possibilities through such questions, or indeed intervene in a physical way; for example by moving an item beyond the reach of a crawling infant. It is worth noting how problem posing, like its companion problem solving, is a fundamental part of learning and doing mathematics (McGrath 2012a; 2012b). Problem posing is creating new problems from old ones, as well as making changes to given problems. What if one of the pieces of information in the problem is changed? Skilful questioning from this starting point leads to problem posing (McGrath 2010). Problem posing presents important thinking challenges. In story contexts we connect to this way of thinking, by playing with story plots we pose new problems.

What if?

If we change something about the story we change something about the mathematics and inversely, if we change something about the mathematics we change something about the story. The original relationship between story and mathematics is changed by asking 'what if?'

Problem solving

Essentially, a problem presents a challenge (McGrath 2010). Problem solving challenges children to use what they already know. Different problems require different strategies to solve them (McGrath 2010). Some of the associated skills for solving problems are: estimating what a reasonable answer should be; recognising patterns; recording data; pictorially representing the problem and checking the answer for reasonableness.

Problem solving is using and applying acquired skills; problem posing is potentially extending knowledge. Therein lies the difference between the two; and problem posing brings possible risk, as we may not know the answer. Brown (2003, p.193) advocates that 'the most effective way is to teach mathematics as a problem-posing-problem-solving cycle of activity'. Marion Walter in discussion with Baxter (2005) advises that 'not all good problem solvers are good problem posers, and vice versa'. This brings us to another relevant point; creating problems for others to solve. In the context of story this could be changing the story in order to prompt new mathematical ideas.

Creating problems

Problem posing encourages curiosity, intellectual activity and sophisticated thinking. Creating problems for others to solve brings posing problems to a higher level; one must take a bird's eye view and be aware of flaws inherent in the structure of the problem (McGrath 2010). This is high-level creative work. Combining the skills of problem solving and problem posing brings children on to creating problems. In the context of story: creating an original story is more challenging than retelling a familiar story or changing some feature of that story.

Polya (1945) advises us that being a problem solver is not enough: problem posing and creating involves thinking on a higher plane beyond applying what one already knows, which is problem solving. Hersh (1998) suggests questions are the driving force and that solving and making problems are at the heart of mathematics. Whereas problem solving is about applying acquired skills, problem posing is about changing something; it is a riskier business.

Creativity is a risky business

Problem posing is a riskier business as it invites creativity. Haylock and Cockburn (2013, p.294) characterise creativity in mathematics as 'thinking flexibly, rather than rigidly, divergently rather than convergently, showing originality and inventiveness, and being prepared to take risks'. Taking risks is important for mathematical creativity. Flexible, divergent, inventive thinking (Haylock & Cockburn 2013) is encouraged, in particular when working with story and oral mathematical storytelling. Uncertainty of play makes this a risky business, as is the uncertainty of oral story. We return to risk in Chapter 6.

A framework to conceptualise mathematics and capture children's mathematical behaviour

Faced with the challenge of framing mathematics, this chapter responds by drawing from a model proposed by Casey (2011; 1999), which helps conceptualise mathematics. Throughout this book, in addition to the theme of joining story and mathematics, an emphasis is placed on children's mathematical behaviour: talking, acting and representing mathematical ideas in drawings. Classroom discussions, observations and extracts from play scenarios elicit children's mathematical behaviours, which are captured using an observational tool combining ideas to conceptualise mathematics proposed by Casey (2011; 1999) and an observational structure for assessment known as learning stories devised by Carr (2001).

Mathematics is complex, involving knowledge, skills, processes and an emotional disposition. I propose we adapt Casey's model (2011; 1999) to help us conceptualise mathematics; to observe children's mathematical behaviour when listening to a story, playing with story-related materials and taking roles as storytellers. Casey considers mathematics broadly as acquisition of: *'facts* and *skills; fluency, curiosity* and *creativity'* (Casey 2011, p.132, italics in original) and as key mathematical methodologies: *'algorithm, conjecture, generalization, isomorphism* and *proof* (Casey 2011, p.132, italics in original). These have been adapted into a list as part of an observational tool based on a format proposed by Carr (2001) (see Figure 1.3).

Koshy (2001) comments on how the acquisition of skills selected by Casey (1999) ensures a balance between the discipline and practice of mathematics. Children need to acquire facts and skills and develop fluency as well as freedom to follow ideas about which they are curious, and a balance between these components should develop a capacity for creativity (Koshy 2001). Fluency with facts is required to operate well with mathematics (Koshy 2001).

Mathematical methodologies proposed by Casey (2011; 1999)

Algorithm: algorithms or procedures or mathematical calculations are essential for mathematics, some of which include addition, subtraction, multiplication and division.

Conjecture: a conjecture is a statement that is followed by checking to find if this is the case (Haylock 2006). A conjecture is 'an assertion the truth of which has not yet been established or checked by the individual making it' (Haylock 2006, p.322). Haylock (2006, p.311) provides an example of a conjecture: 91 is a prime number but demonstrates that by checking, this conjecture is found to be incorrect as 91 can be divided by 7 and 13. A prime number can only be divided by itself and one, but 91 can be divided by 1, 91, 7 and 13. In this case the conjecture that 91 is a prime number is found to be untrue.

A child's disposition towards learning mathematics is important: 'Above all, of great importance in mathematics is the attribute of developing a "what if?" learning disposition' (Pound & Lee, 2011, p.9). The disposition to think 'what if?' is at the heart of problem solving and is referred to as conjectural thinking by Pound and Lee (2011). 'What if?' is a conjectural question, which encourages problem posing and solving. Sheffield (1999, cited by Casey 2011) recommends asking: what if I change one or more parts of the problem? Watson and Mason (1998, cited by Casey 2011) state that questions such as 'what if?' provoke children into becoming aware of mathematical possibilities. Possibility thinking is framed by the 'what if?' question and is central to creative work with mathematical story. I refer to Pound and Lee's (2011) interpretation of 'what if?' as a conjectural question that is posed and solved through story-related thinking. This small question lies at the heart of creative thinking (Craft 2001; Haylock & Cockburn 2013; Pound & Lee 2011; Sheffield 1999, cited by Casey 2011; Watson & Mason 1998, cited by Casey 2011) and can be the key we turn when thinking of mathematical ideas through story.

Generalising: in life, it is wise not to generalise as this can lead to making misplaced assumptions. Generalising is about making general or broad statements (Fairclough 2011). In mathematics, it is important to see patterns, to make general statements that articulate pattern, and to explain why this is so. In articulating a generalisation children are making one statement that is true about a number of specific cases (Haylock & Cockburn 2013). Haylock and Cockburn describe how generalisations are statements 'in which there is reference to something that is *always* the case. As soon as children begin to put words such as *each, every, any, all, always, whenever* and *if . . . then* into their observations they are generalizing' (2013, p.297; italics in original). These words are markers of children reasoning in a way that is characteristic of thinking mathematically (Haylock & Cockburn 2013). One of our challenges as educators is to encourage children to see patterns and make connections and generalisations about mathematical ideas.

Questions to prompt describing or generalising about a pattern

What is the pattern in the story?

Does that happen every time?

What do you think will happen next?

What pattern are you using or thinking about?

How can you check that (using story-related props)?

(adapted from Haylock & Cockburn 2013, p.299)

Generalisations in mathematics come from seeing patterns. Frobisher *et al.* (1999, p.240) describe how '[r]elationships and the establishment and recording of general statements about numbers have their foundations in pattern'. Frobisher *et al.* (1999, p.266) highlight how '[c]hildren's growing grasp of addition, subtraction, multiplication and division may be greatly helped by drawing attention to and building on patterns'. Seeing pattern in subtraction allows children to make predictions: if $10 - 2 = 8$ what will $10 - 8$ be? Frobisher *et al.* explain that 'Ultimately, the patterns children find and study can lead to powerful ideas such as generalisations and algebraic formulae' (1999, p.244). Algebraic representations express pattern in general terms.

Trying several examples is encouraged by Casey (2011) as a way of generalising and arriving at a proof; for example, that 'the sum of two consecutive numbers is always odd' (Casey 2011, p.132). The example below shows how this idea can be represented in a general way:

The sum of two consecutive numbers is always odd

If the first number is n then the next number is n + 1

The sum of two consecutive numbers is n + (n + 1)

This can be represented as 2n + 1

As 2n is double n, which must be even, then 2n + 1, the number after 2n, must be odd

The general pattern is expressed algebraically as n + (n + 1) = 2n + 1

(Casey 2011, p.133)

A story can repeat a sequence that is essentially trying out a different example each time. Retelling the story employs more examples, and at some stage it may be appropriate to articulate a pattern and a generalisation. It might be that children use the language of the story to describe the mathematical pattern – a point we return to in later chapters.

Proof: proving is about convincing a sceptic that the generalisation really must be true in all cases (Haylock & Cockburn 2013, p.303), though primary school children are not expected to prove they can formulate simple explanations (Haylock & Cockburn 2013). Children may well use the context of the story to explain mathematical ideas, a point we also return to in Chapter 6.

Children should be encouraged to articulate patterns. There are two potential ways children can be encouraged to do this: to describe what changes, and to describe what stays the same (Haylock & Cockburn 2013). Description about pattern enables children to predict or generalise about what will happen next. Drawing out explanations about what happens every time is getting children to think like mathematicians: to generalise. Frobisher *et al.* (1999) advise that children not only describe the pattern in words as a generalisation but explain why this is so.

Questions to prompt explanations about generalisations

Can you explain?

Why does that happen?

What is going on?

(Haylock & Cockburn 2013, p.303)

Isomorphism: Casey (2011) attaches importance to this component of his model. He describes detecting isomorphism as seeing that different situations share a common mathematical structure: making connections between different contexts requiring the same mathematical skills. The same solution works for two different situations or contextualised problems. By providing a play opportunity with props following a mathematical story, children think about the mathematical story in a different context. In some instances this opens out to applying the mathematical idea of the story in a play context. This is a different take on what Casey (2011; 1999) intends: we adapt his idea of isomorphism; to children taking mathematical ideas heard in a story; to play contexts where children author mathematical narratives themselves.

There are other mathematical processes, some of which are referred to by Casey (2011, p.135) outside of his model, and others observed more generally as children play: communicating (listening, talking, showing); counting; corresponding (one to one correspondence); classifying and sorting; matching; symbolising (using symbols); estimating; reasoning; working systematically; justifying and checking; sequencing and patterning; reflecting and recording. Number relationships include number bonds; subtraction complements; multiples of; doubling. Number complements are important in order that children are flexible with number facts: such as '[t]he ten-complement of a single-digit number is what you need to add to make it up to 10' (Haylock & Cockburn 2013, p.164); and they can be developed further to encourage instant recall of facts up to 20 and beyond.

Mathematical errors and utterances

Carr (2001, p.xiii) considers errors as a way to work out what went wrong and that these are a source of new learning. I include 'mathematical errors' in the observational tool because I find it fascinating to observe how children correct errors; how adults make and avoid correcting errors (sometimes these go unnoticed) and how errors present opportunities that can be returned to if missed, but reflected upon. Children in the project correct errors when counting by employing strategies such as lining ladybird spots up, checking or getting another child to count. I also include a focus on 'mathematical utterances' because I am interested in expressions children use, particularly when using story language to explain mathematical ideas.

An observational tool to capture children's mathematical behaviour (Figure 1.3)

This observational tool essentially tabulates aspects of mathematics so that we can take on the challenge of capturing children's mathematical behaviour. A narrative description of the child is recorded and then mapped against ideas relating to mathematics, using arrows or highlighting. I recommend that a dictaphone is used to record the child at play or retelling mathematical stories and that both the audio recording and the observation notes are shared with children, colleagues and parents.

The tool can be modified and used for three purposes: to conceptualise mathematics, to examine the quality of the mathematical experience (whole class oral story, small group oral story, children playing with story-related props) and to capture children's mathematical behaviours (talking, acting, representing). This tool is used in Chapter 3: we observe a child retelling 'Ladybird on a Leaf' using story-related props in a playful and purposeful way (Figure 1.4). This observational tool is intended for adults in practice who need a manageable way of seeing a child's behaviour through a mathematical lens. The observational tool is applied in Chapter 3. A copy of this observational format is available in Appendix 1.

Conclusion

'No Problem!' (Browne & Parkins 1993) is chosen as an opening to this chapter because the story of how Mouse comes to have an aeroplane contextualises mathematical problem solving strategies. The story follows a problem posing, problem solving sequence. 'No Problem!' shows a harmonious relationship between the story of Mouse and mathematical problem solving strategies. In this story, children experience the wonder of mathematical problem solving, connections exist between mathematics and imaginative ideas of the story, and somehow the story helps make sense of an imaginary world of animals, with different dispositions, solving a problem in creative ways. Shrew follows instructions systematically and makes an aeroplane. By allowing children to solve problems in more than one fixed way, we encourage flexible thinking, explore multiple ways of reasoning and consider connections among strategies.

Mathematical observation

Mathematical features	Narrative description
Conjecturing: 'What if?' (problem posing)	
Algorithm (for example, adding, subtracting, multiplying, dividing)	
Mathematical utterances (mathematical words)	
Mathematical facts	
Generalisation (making mathematical connections, seeing patterns)	
Mathematical mistakes or misunderstandings	
Transferring mathematical ideas to play contexts	
Curiosity (within mathematical context)	
Fluency (ease of use of mathematical ideas)	

Title	Age of child in years and months	Gender	Context	Initials of observer	Date	Audio recorded reference

Prompts	Observer comments
Transfer of mathematical ideas to context such as play or retelling stories	
Use of props	
Connection to original story heard	
Extending ideas	
Follow up	

Outcome of discussion with child	Outcome of discussion with parent

Figure 1.3 An observational tool to capture children's mathematical behaviour based on the format for Learning Stories (Carr 2001).

Figure 1.4 Jake retelling 'Ladybird on a Leaf' using a sugar paper ladybird and spots.

This chapter explores the relationship between problem posing and problem solving. Problem posing and problem solving are companions but are different: the relationship between problem posing and problem solving could be described as like old slippers, which need to be stepped into as a pair. Problem posing and solving is a common thread connecting mathematics and story.

Mental strategies based on imaginative mathematical images of story words and props develop confidence in manipulating numbers and articulating patterns. We consider the importance of encouraging children to articulate these patterns and make generalisations about mathematical ideas using story language, a point we will return to in Chapter 6.

It is difficult to set about conceptualising mathematics. The proposed observational tool helps us to capture children's mathematical behavior when listening to story, playing with story-related props, and retelling oral mathematical stories. Adults can work with story in such a way that it opens out mathematical understanding for young children. Relationships between story and mathematical ideas can be unfolded to support children's understanding, like a flower opening out.

Story

... we look at the world in terms of stories all the time. They are the most natural way in which we structure our descriptions of the world around us.

(Booker 2004, p.573)

The aims of this chapter are to:

- establish a shared understanding of the words: 'discourse', 'narrative', 'plot' and 'story'
- gain insight into story structure: components and qualities of stories
- consider story as a pedagogical tool to teach mathematics.

'Handa's Surprise'

Handa sets off with seven exotic fruits in a basket on her head for her friend Akeyo. One at a time each piece of fruit is taken by one of seven different animals:

'Handa put seven delicious fruits in a basket for her friend, Akeyo.
She will be surprised, thought Handa as she set off for Akeyo's village.
I wonder which fruit she'll like best?
Will she like the soft yellow banana . . .
or the sweet-smelling guava?
Will she like the round juicy orange . . .
or the ripe red mango?
Will she like the spiky-leaved pineapple . . .
the creamy green avocado . . .
or the tangy purple passion-fruit?
Which fruit will Akeyo like best?'

A tethered goat escapes and knocks into a tree, dropping tangerines into
Handa's empty basket:
' "Hello, Akeyo", said Handa. "I've brought you a surprise."
"Tangerines!" said Akeyo. "My favourite fruit."
"TANGERINES?" said Handa. "That *is* a surprise!" '

(Browne 1998)

Figure 2.1 A monkey takes a banana from Handa's basket of seven fruits (Browne 1998).
Copyright © 1994 Eileen Browne. From 'Handa's Surprise' by Eileen Browne. Reproduced by
permission of Walker Books Ltd, London SE11 5HJ www.walker.co.uk

Introduction

It seems too obvious to pause to think about what the word 'story' means, but it is the obvious that eludes us. Understanding the word 'story' deserves attention, particularly if we are to work with it as a creative approach to teach mathematics.

If you were to create a story for children, you might think about a place and pose a problem for a character to solve. You would think of why the character needs to solve the problem. There would be an order to the sequence of events: the question 'what then?' would help you sequence the story. Thinking in this sequential way could be considered mathematical.

Connections between story and mathematics exist on at least three levels: first, story follows a sequence and as such can be viewed as mathematical; second, the problem posing, problem solving tendency of story characters runs along a mathematical type of thinking track; third, the essence of a story can be richly mathematical if we choose to seek this out (McGrath 2010). Stories such as 'The Doorbell Rang' (Hutchins 1986), 'The Giant Jam Sandwich' (Lord & Burroway 1972) and 'Handa's Surprise' (Browne 1998) are rich with mathematical opportunity. When I explain to author and illustrator Eileen Browne the idea of seeing mathematical opportunity in picture books, she describes her books 'as inadvertently having mathematical threads running through them' (Browne 2013). Stories such as 'Handa's Surprise' are accidentally mathematical and not written with this intention, but can, for example with this story, connect children to thinking about 'one less than': each time an animal takes a fruit there is one less; one less than seven is six, one less than six is five and so on. When we tease out the relationships between story and mathematics, we achieve insight into how best to use story to support mathematical thinking.

One of the aims of this chapter is to define the words 'narrative', 'plot', 'story' and 'discourse', so that these words can be understood in a way that promotes story as a pedagogical tool to teach mathematics. We want to understand something about the structure and qualities of stories so that we are equipped to move between text and oral modes of story, and possibly to create our own stories.

Establishing a shared understanding of words

It is important to define words used to represent concepts so that we share an understanding of what these words mean, we shed assumptions about what words mean and we open out new imaginings or possibilities.

Commonly used words can be deceptively difficult to define. Bal (1985, cited in McQuillan 2000, p.82) makes the point that it is important to clarify concepts we work with. Bal adds that concepts can be used so often that users understand them differently: 'Such is the case with very common and seemingly obvious notions such as *literature, text, narrative,* and *poem*' (Bal 1985, cited in McQuillan 2000, p.82, italics in original). I suggest that, like 'play' and 'mathematics', the notion of 'story' is difficult to define. One way of agreeing on the meaning of concepts is to define the words describing them.

Story shape: sequence and pattern

Booker (2004) describes how stories create 'strange sequences' of mental images in our minds. Stories call upon 'our ability to "imagine", to bring up to our conscious perception the images of things which are not actually in front of our eyes' (Booker 2004, p.3). Beyond this sequence of images there is an overall pattern to story. The shape of a story unfolds around a general pattern and the intention is that this pattern or structure gives a 'satisfactory shape to a story' (Booker 2004, p.4). Stories throughout history share similar patterns. Story is composed of a sequence of images, bound by a plot that, if well structured, has a satisfactory shape.

Discourse

Narratology is the theory of narrative texts and delves into distinguishing between discourse and story. McQuillan (2000, p.317) explains that '[d]iscourse consists of both the medium (written, oral, cinematic) and the form (the order of presentation, the point of view, the narrator, etc.)'. Story can be expressed through written, oral or screen media and from different perspectives. Story takes on different forms depending on how it is presented.

If we keep in our mind the idea that story is a sequence of events and that discourse is the medium through which a story is expressed, we share an understanding about these two words; in later chapters we rely less on written and more on oral discourse as we work with oral mathematical stories.

Narrative

What is our understanding of narrative? This is a slippery term that, in the field of narrative theory, remains 'unstable' (McQuillan 2000). Lyotard (1984; 1992, cited in McQuillan 2000, p.323) identifies that narrative is a mode of knowledge, from the Latin root 'gnarus', 'knowing'. Written text and oral narrative are modes of knowledge that we wish to use to promote mathematical ideas. McQuillan (2000, p.323) states how 'narratives define the possibilities of knowledge and, hence, action in any given society'; we are concerned with the possibility of mathematical knowledge and action in early years settings and primary school classrooms of contemporary society.

Plot

The driving force behind the sequence of events of story is the plot; the engine that pulls the connecting carriages of the train. One way of defining plot is to think of it

Drawing definitions together

If 'oral' is a form of discourse, 'narrative' a mode of knowledge, 'story' a sequence of events, then 'oral narrative story' extends to 'oral mathematical narrative story'. We combine words to create phrases such as 'oral story', or 'oral narrative story', or 'oral mathematical story' to establish shared understanding.

as the main events of a narrative; a compression of the sequence of events. However, again there is a subtlety to consider. Story is determined by sequence or chronology, and plot by consequence or causality (McQuillan 2000, p.325). A story sequence can be teased out with a 'what then?' question, whereas plot needs a 'why?' question to realise the difference.

Before we take up the idea of playing with the plot of a story we tease out the meaning of plot by looking at the relationship between narrative and story. In life we are immersed in narratives as we catch snippets of other people's conversations, listen to the news and so on. However, '[w]hile all stories are narratives (a recounting of events), not all narratives are stories' (McQuillan 2000, p.328); the difference is fixing a story with a plot. Forrester (1963, cited in McQuillan 2000, p.45) confirms that '[w]e have defined a story as a narrative of events arranged in their time-sequence. A plot is also a narrative of events, the emphasis falling on causality'. The plot is a sequence, but there is an added aspect of cause as to why the sequence happens. Forrester (1963, cited in McQuillan 2000, p.45) suggests the 'and then?' question relies on curiosity in the listener; the plot question 'why?' relies on memory and intelligence. A story has a plot, an account has no plot, but both are narratives.

Three story-related questions to keep in mind:

the 'and then?' question: story sequence

the 'why?' question: story plot

the 'what if?' question: playing with plot to prompt mathematical thinking.

Story as a form of art

After defining story-related words 'discourse', 'narrative' amd 'plot', we might remain dissatisfied and continue to ask: what is story, really? Bryant (1947, p.20) suggests 'a story is essentially and primarily a work of art, and its chief function must be sought in the line of the uses of art', such function being to give pleasure. Bryant (1947) holds a firm view that the purpose of a story should be a child's pleasure over his instruction. Any intention to use story to teach mathematics needs to preserve pleasure; finding a balance between the pleasures of art and mathematical ideas demands careful crafting.

A child's perspective describing story experiences

When I ask a six-year-old child to describe what happens when they read a story or listen to a story told orally, they comment:

> About a picture book . . .
> 'You can see the pictures. So that's one person's imagination. You can see the pictures from one person's imagination.'
> About a story read with no pictures . . .
> 'You just imagine it.'
> About a story told (a story from my head) . . .
> 'It's better because you can imagine your own pictures.'

A theoretical perspective describing story experience:

> 'Were not the excitement and assurance of that experience precisely the result of the mystery of such a fusion? You were listening. You were in the story. You were in the words of the story-teller. You were no longer your single self; you were, thanks to the story, *everyone it concerned*.'
> (Berger & Mohr 1982, cited in McQuillan 2000, p.172, italics in original)

Structure

Bruner (1986, p.21) suggests that what we seek in structure is how to integrate plight, characters and consciousness: the story 'requires an uneven distribution of underlying consciousness among the characters with respect to the plight'. Characters have different levels of awareness of the problem at the heart of a story plot. Handa is not aware of the fruit being taken from her basket and being replaced by tangerines because a goat knocks into a tree. Bruner (1986, p.21) suggests that '[w]hat gives the story its unity is the manner in which plight, characters, and consciousness interact to yield a structure that has a start, a development, and a "sense of an ending" '. Story is shaped by these interactions.

Insight into story structure: components and qualities of stories

Qualities of successful stories for children

We now look at qualities of story with a view to furnishing ourselves with a frame of reference to use when dismantling, rebuilding or creating stories. Bryant (1947) focuses on three successful stories to draw out these traits: 'The Three Little Pigs'; 'The Three Bears'; and 'The Old Woman and her Pig', and proposes three qualities as follows:

Qualities of successful children's stories

Each step of a story is an event:

> 'Something happens all the time. Every step in each story is an event. There is no time spent in explanation, description, or telling how people felt; the stories tell what people did, and what they said. And the events are the links of a sequence of the closest kind; in point of time and of cause they follow as immediately as it is possible for events to follow. There are no gaps, and no complications of plot requiring a return on the road' (Bryant 1947, p.58).

Simplicity connects a child and story worlds:

> 'As you run over the little stories you will see that each event presents a distinct picture to the imagination, and that these pictures are made out of very simple elements. The elements are either familiar to the child or analogous to familiar ones. Each object and happening is very like everyday, yet touched with a subtle difference, rich in mystery' (Bryant 1947, p.58).

Repetition:

> 'Still a third characteristic common to the stories quoted is a certain amount of repetition' (Bryant 1947, p.59).

If we take the example of 'Goldilocks and the Three Bears' we find that for young children, stories work best when each sequence is closely associated with the story. There is simplicity in the sequence of events and there is a lifelikeness of bears eating porridge, sitting on chairs and sleeping in beds, which a child relates to. The detail is simple and mysterious but offers familiarity to a child. There are parallels between the world of bears and ordinary life. For young children, the repetition of a phrase and/or action serves to hook their attention (Bryant 1947). This repetitive phrase serves to elicit confidence and reconnect children if attention strays.

Story structure: components and qualities

To draw together the components of story we could summarise as follows: a story is a series of events, taking place over time, which involve a character who is posed with a problem (plight), in a particular location or place, and will be told from a particular point of view. The character often has a consciousness about the problem and it is the connecting of problem, character and their awareness or consciousness that shapes the story (Bruner 1986). The events will be sequenced into a beginning, middle and end. To ensure success, each step or piece of the story is an event; through simple detail, a child connects between parallel worlds of a story and his or her own experience (the three bears sit on chairs, eat with spoons and sleep in beds); repetition draws on a child's confidence and concentration. These qualities will need to feature alongside mathematical ideas in a way that preserves the story as an art form (Bryant 1947).

From these points we put together a story profile (Appendix 2) to help us think about story and the components and qualities that appeal to children. This profile can be used to dismantle a story so that we can set out the parts, like Shrew in 'No Problem!' (Browne & Parkins 1993). There is story profile for 'Handa's Surprise' in Appendix 3.

This profile can be used to create original stories. As well as this tool there are three key questions to ask when creating original stories:

Threefold test to our own story creations:

Are they full of action, in close natural sequence?

Are their images simple without being humdrum?

Are they repetitive?

(Bryant 1947)

Story as a pedagogical tool to teach mathematics

As individuals we are part of a culture that has evolved through history and, as Bruner states: 'It can never be the case that there is a "self" independent of one's cultural-historical existence' (1986, p. 67). Our culture and the stories of that culture are part of our existence. We are nurtured by stories of the culture we are born to; we are neither free from our genes or our changing culture (Bruner 1986). Children are shaped by the stories of their culture.

Story sheds light on our human existence, as Booker (2004, p.8) explains: 'on our psychology; on morality; on the patterns of history and politics, and the nature of religion; on the underlying pattern and purpose of our individual lives'. Adults and children look to stories to understand more about ourselves as we internally calibrate against the world around us.

Children work hard to make sense of the world they are born into. Children come to realise that 'many worlds are possible, that meaning and reality are created and not discovered, that negotiation is the art of constructing new meanings by which individuals can regulate their relations with each other' (Bruner 1986, p.149). A child's understanding about their culture is constructed through the stories they hear.

Children construct mathematical understanding

The rationale for teaching mathematics through story is to support the construction of mathematical understanding; children sense a mathematical pattern and experience mathematics. After hearing a story several times patterns may be articulated, described in words and generalised imaginatively. Children organise and internalise mathematical ideas of story and construct meaning.

Story offers an alternative way of teaching mathematics. Research points to the value of using both story and play pedagogical approaches:

> In a climate when the curriculum for mathematics sessions may be fairly prescribed, teachers will be encouraged to note the evidence that stories and play prove to be important and effective ways of enhancing young children's appreciation of mathematical concepts.
>
> (Haylock & Cockburn 2013, p.86)

A story approach to teaching mathematics offers something different for both adult and learner. There is a satisfaction in reading, telling or creating stories. This experience is mutually rewarding for both educators and children.

Stories suggested in this book differ from stylised mathematical stories. Stories referred to in this book generally have, at their heart, a *plot*, so that it is a genuine story experience. They are not just narratives to transport mathematics. When a story becomes a narrative we need to draw in the reins and reshape the experience so that it returns to being a *genuine* story experience. Working with published quality children's literature might help us to avoid falling into the trap of over stylising mathematical content. We can work outwards from these published stories, playing with plot, before creating well balanced original material.

Zone of Proximal Development (ZPD)

Vygotsky places value on children learning from adults and more capable peers when he proposes the concept of the Zone of Proximal Development (ZPD):

> It is the distance between the actual developmental level as determined by independent problem solving and the level of potential development as determined through problem solving under adult guidance or in collaboration with more capable peers.
>
> (Vygotsky 1978 p.86)

Rogoff refers to Vygotsky's sociocultural theory (1978), noting how cognitive development relies on people learning to employ cultural tools for literacy and mathematical thinking through the help of others more experienced with these tools (Rogoff 2003, p.237). Rogoff refers to adult intervention in terms of guided participation, describing how 'in interactions within the ZPD, children learn to use the intellectual tools of their community, including literacy, number systems, language, and tools for remembering and planning' (2003, p.282). The Zone of Proximal Development, theorised by Vygotsky (1978), can be supported with adult intervention through story in a mathematical developmental context.

Story plays a role in supporting children's cognitive development. The challenge will be working with story in such a way that mathematical functions in an embryonic state are nurtured (Vygotsky 1978). The intention of this book is to encourage adults to guide children's mathematical development through story.

Oral story

Schiro (2004) describes the importance of stories in people's lives and refers to story as a 'primal act of mind'. In the past, storytellers combined education with story, and this is still the case in certain cultures (Rogoff 2003). Story is a way of understanding others and ourselves. Schiro (2004, p.53) describes how 'stories allow the story teller to speak to children (while passing on cultural information, attitudes, and values) in a way and on a level that is uniquely suited to children's way of making meaning'. Using oral story as a way to communicate ideas draws on a long tradition; using oral story to communicate mathematical ideas is less charted.

Oral storytelling brings a unique experience to educator and child. Grugeon and Gardner explain the difference between reading and telling a story, stating: 'reading is a process of sharing and interpreting a text that someone else has produced, but telling a story is a unique and personal performance' (2000, p.2). Schiro (2004, p.55) describes how 'the orally delivered story is different because the human voice is a different medium from the written word'. Humpty Dumpty, a traditional Nursery Rhyme, inspires Little Lumpty, a character in a picture book, and retelling this printed story orally brings out something different: 'in its retelling, through the medium of a different voice, it will take on new resonances' (Grugeon & Gardner 2000, p.121). I return to this experience of telling the story of Little Lumpty to facilitate the mathematical idea of counting in multiples of two in Chapter 5.

One of the educators featured in Schiro's (2004, p.104) work describes a different energy in the room when she tells story orally, and refers to the 'intrinsic power of an oral story'. Oral storytelling can be a powerful experience. When educators read a prescribed story they can remain separate (Schiro 2004); when educators create oral story, a more intimate relationship with both the story and the audience develops. Schiro (2004) compares educators employing children's storybooks to engaging in oral storytelling, and describes how the storyteller is free from text, needs to be spontaneous, has a closer connection with their audience and has a personal consciousness. There is an inherent freedom in oral story, as '[t]elling sets you free from the written text and allows you to alter and add to the original version and to adapt it to the needs of your audience' (Grugeon & Gardner 2000, p.2). There is scope to include an audience in oral story and to draw from unique interactions. This flexibility of oral storytelling can be exploited to connect story and mathematical ideas.

Imagination

Egan (1988) considers that imagination is a neglected tool of learning. Egan (1988, p.18) suggests that we 'rethink our teaching practices and curricula with a more balanced appreciation of children's intellectual capacities', placing imagination in a more prominent position. Imagination is difficult to grasp, and as such there is little educational research that focuses on it (Egan 1988). In fact, Egan argues that some of the principles concerning teaching and curricula 'suppress children's imagination and undermine some of its potential educational uses' (1988, p.6). Schiro (2004, p.77) holds the view that '[o]ne of the most powerful parts of children's intellectual life is their imaginative and fantasizing capability'. Schiro (2004, p.46) describes the intention behind oral storytelling as an attempt to personalise and contextualise mathematics in imaginative ways. Schiro expresses the view that '[f]antasy, imagination, intuition, emotion, and playfulness are at the centre of the instructional process' (2004, p.46), and advises employing oral story to support children's mathematical development.

Children can learn in abstract ways

Egan (1988) challenges the principle that children need to move from the concrete to the abstract using the idea of how children deal with abstract fantasy stories. Egan identifies the principle of how 'young children's active manipulation of concrete objects should precede abstract or symbolic learning' (1988, p.6) but questions 'whether children learn *everything* best from such experiences. Can they learn *only* from such experiences? Are there things that *cannot* be learned from such experiences?' (italics in original, 1988, p.8). Egan concludes that 'even though young children might not articulate abstract terms and have difficulty with *certain kinds* of abstract concepts, it is not true that abstract concepts in general are difficult for young children' (italics in original, 1988, p.10). Egan (1988) advocates that children's intellectual development is not totally about starting from the concrete before moving to the abstract, proposing that children relate well to the abstract ideas of story.

Children's conceptual abilities are evident in how they manage and relate to rhythm of stories (Egan 1988). Oral storytelling transforms abstract, objective, deductive

Figure 2.2 Ikran playfully dramatises 'Handa's Surprise'.

mathematics into a world of imagination and emotions (Schiro 2004) and, through the abstract ideas of story, children can access abstract mathematical ideas.

Oral mathematical story promotes mathematical language, starting with the articulation of the problem and ending with an expression of the idea. Schiro (2004) states how children relearn mathematical language through story. Our challenge as storytellers is to ensure that mathematical vocabulary is secure in a story structure. Pratt explains how 'vocabulary is picked up through its use, not before its use, in a dynamic relationship between using words and understanding the associated ideas' (2006, p.27). This is evident in the later chapters where children use the vocabulary of story with related materials to express mathematical ideas.

Schiro (2004) advocates that educators of mathematics explore the 'instructional power of oral stories' and encourages adults to use their creativity, presenting stories from within themselves. Oral storytelling allows teachers to personalise mathematics and connect it to their own creativity (Schiro 2004). Later chapters adapt published stories that are told to children in ways that generate creative mathematical dialogue. In keeping with Schiro's view (2004), oral story is suggested as a way of complementing other pedagogic choices and is not the salvation of mathematics education.

Conclusion

This chapter clarifies terms so that we share a common understanding of the meaning of story-related words. We bring story-associated words together to make phrases: oral (discourse medium) mathematical narrative (mode of knowledge) story (sequence bound by plot); oral mathematical narrative story; or, more simply, oral mathematical story.

Insight into what makes a successful story will help when selecting, adapting and creating stories. For young children stories need to be structured such that each step is an event, some simple detail of the story connects children to this other world and repetitive phrases and actions hook children in.

I propose that story offers mathematical opportunity; that children's literature is often accidentally mathematical. Our intention is to capitalise on mathematical opportunity in story; disturb relationships between story and mathematics; connect other mathematical ideas to story and see mathematical ideas beyond story. Adults can provide guided participation and scaffold children's mathematical development through story. For educationalists, story is a pedagogical tool to engage children mathematically. For children, story is a world through which mathematics can be imagined (see Figure 2.2).

Threading play in a mathematical way

In play thought is separated from objects and action arises from ideas rather than from things: a piece of wood begins to be a doll and a stick becomes a horse.

(Vygotsky 1978, p.97)

This chapter aims to explore three themes:

- play as implicitly mathematical
- children expressing explicit mathematical ideas in play
- children as mathematical narrative authors in play.

'Teremok' adapted from a Russian tale (versions of the story are available in Arnold 1994; Ransome 2003)

This is a story about a little hut in a wood. A small cat arrives at the clearing. The cat looks in front of the hut, behind the hut, on top, next to the hut and under the hut and then wonders what's inside the hut? He begins to knock: 'Knock, knock, knock, Tere-teremok, who will answer when I knock?' No one answers and so he climbs inside and falls asleep. A bee arrives to the clearing and is curious about the hut and decides to knock: 'Knock, knock, knock, Tere-teremok, who will answer when I knock?' The cat answers and the bee goes inside to sleep. Other animals arrive and each time there is a knock the last animal in opens the door to the latest arrival. Then there is the sound of big, booming steps. The bear looks in front, behind, on top of, next to and under the hut curious to know what is inside the little hut. The bear can tell he won't fit in and can be heard deciding to sit on top of the hut. The animals inside panic and run from the hut one by one in the order of last in first out. The bear decides against sitting on top of the little hut in the wood.

(Brown 2013a)

Introduction

This chapter starts with a description of ideas connecting mathematics and play. We look at play through a mathematical lens: problem posing and problem solving in play is mathematical. Children listen to an oral story version of the traditional Russian tale 'Teremok', which has been rewritten as a children's picture book by Arnold (1994) and is similar to a story titled 'Who Lived in the Skull?' which features as part of a collection by Ransome (2003). Children listen to the story being retold by storyteller Paula Brown and are later observed playing with loosely associated props. Children express some of the mathematical ideas of Teremok in play.

A boy listens to a story about a ladybird on a leaf and is observed playing in a way which retells the story using his own choice of number and number patterns. The observational tool set out in Chapter 1 captures this child's mathematical behaviour. Play is seen as implicitly mathematical in the way children pose and solve problems, create imaginary worlds, symbolise abstract ideas and express explicit story-related mathematical ideas.

The problem posing and solving theme of this chapter is reflected in the words of Pound and Lee as they describe how:

Children at play will try things out, refine them, come back to them, look at them from another angle, bring in other children to support the idea they are exploring, change roles and find reasons and solutions to problems that seem insurmountable.

(Pound & Lee 2011, p.64)

These features of children's approach to play are comparable to those required for mathematical understanding (Pound & Lee 2011). The aim of this chapter is to see play in a mathematical way and to be able to interpret children's play behaviour in this way.

Play as implicitly mathematical

Children thread ideas through their play narratives in imaginative ways. There is immediacy of thought, word and action, which make threads of play wiry and alive. It is as if in play children's ideas search out direction and are redirected, like the antennae of an insect exploring new territory. A child does not know in advance where these play ideas will go: they stretch up and out, into the present moment, taking shape as they go.

Play: tip of immediate thinking

If you join and play alongside a child you sense this immediacy of play. If as an adult you allow a child to lead you in imaginary play, it is as if you are pulled along by a thread. The child is pulling on this thread and being pulled by the uncertainty of what happens next. The child is at the tip of immediate thinking when playing in this way. An attitude of mind is required when playing in this way: an attitude open to possibility (Craft 2001). There is no certainty and no predetermined end.

Possibility thinking of play: what if?

At the heart of creativity is possibility thinking, which drives innovation. Craft (2001) describes innovation as a quality of creativity. Craft (2001, p.91) suggests that creative or imaginative approaches include questioning with 'what if?' as an expression of possibility thinking. Play is about possibility thinking. In play children test out possibilities of props. 'What if?' as a conjectural question of story and mathematics features also in play. What if this plastic plate is a steering wheel? What if this red blanket is the sea? When we watch a child play we see a kaleidoscopic process (Ginnis & Ginnis 2006): a child turns his or her ideas in and in, to change and change, out and out, as new ideas form. Some play scenarios slow this turning down, while a child thinks deeply.

Abstract thought

Vygotsky considers that a child's creation of imaginary situations is a way of developing abstract thought: 'From the point of view of development, creating an imaginary situation can be regarded as a means of developing abstract thought' (Vygotsky 1978, p.103). In creating imaginary situations children select materials to represent abstract ideas for these imaginary worlds.

Play for Tomorrow

I show Early Childhood foundation degree students each year a recording of a television documentary titled 'Play for Tomorrow'. Colwyn Trevarthen shows a video clip of children playing. He describes how a child decides the inside of a toilet roll is a telescope. He is fascinated about how the children playing agree it is a telescope. The toilet roll tube becomes a telescope and that is that. In this play scenario, children agree this alternative meaning.

(Play for Tomorrow 1991)

35

Children as mathematical narrative authors

Children are authors when they play: authors of ideas. The narrative of play can differ from that of story as a child's play may not have the problem or tension of a plot as described in Chapter 2. Play may be more of a narrative account, a stream of thoughts, connected to words, connected to actions in an immediate way. This narrative may not be bound by plot, but sometimes is: it is often more fluid and less framed by structure. Children are authors of these play narratives. Children are sometimes mathematical narrative authors in play.

Mathematical thinking implicit in play: problem posing and problem solving

In Chapter 1, problem posing is found to be a companion for problem solving. We now consider how children's play is about problem posing and problem solving. Children at play problem pose and problem solve in a natural mathematical way; children are asking 'what if?' even if they are too young to articulate these words.

A playful attitude: relationships between problem posing, problem solving and play

Children's playful dispositions lead them to look for new problems, alternative methods, and novel solutions. The young child is a natural problem seeker (Pound 2008). Play poses problems, which are tested and overcome in a natural way (McGrath 2010, p.204). We could extend Pound's statement (2006, p.82) that '[i]n their play children learn early a number of thinking skills which are vital to the development of mathematical thinking', to say that play is thinking in a mathematical way: play is mathematical. Playful attitudes promote creativity, both in children and in adults who play.

Examples of problem posing and problem solving in every day play

It is fascinating to see the natural fitting together of problem posing and problem solving in play scenarios. Some brief accounts of children playing in this mathematical way follow.

By providing loosely or more closely associated story props we promote different play possibilities. Though play is unpredictable there is a possibility that not only will children play in a mathematical way, but that play may express explicit mathematical ideas of stories.

Scenario one: matching yellow three hole pieces

Molly Mae, aged one year, throws pieces of Numicon, liking the clatter on a wooden floor. She finds a yellow L-shaped three-hole piece and when she finds a matching piece she holds both up as if she knows this is a pair. There are no words but a sense that she looks for a possible yellow match as she repeats this action three times.

Scenario two: dividing sheep into pens

'Floss' by Kim Lewis (1992), a story about a sheepdog, is read to a three-year-old child. In play a farm is created with a sheep dog, 24 sheep and wooden blocks. The child lines up the sheep and separates 24 sheep into four pens.

Scenario three: creating an imaginary camper van

A camper van is created by deciding on the positioning and arrangement of cushions, a blanket, a cardboard box and chairs. A sequence of story is layered by a five-year-old child, who enacts travelling, eating and sleeping. Time is spent arranging and testing out different ways before arriving at satisfactory solutions: the distance between chairs is adjusted so that a red blanket stays on top. A tube of poster paint on a nearby art table is imagined as ketchup and is packed in the van.

Children expressing explicit mathematical ideas in play

When children are deep in play they are creating, enquiring, reasoning, processing information, evaluating and reflecting (Ginnis & Ginnis 2006). Children connect ideas in play. Intuition, reasoning, analysis and logic integrate in play (Ginnis & Ginnis 2006). Mathematical thinking is implicit in play; it is also a way children express mathematics explicitly. I observe two children playing after Paula Brown, a storyteller, tells 'Teremok' to a class of 30 four- and five-year-olds (Brown 2013a). One of the mathematical themes of this storytelling is positional language and another is about capacity. The play situation is supported with two vegetable boxes and soft animal toys.

Play scenario following 'Teremok'

Corey and Olivia play with large and small vegetable boxes and a collection of soft animal toys. Below is an extract from the play scenario that relates to 'Teremok' before the play becomes about pirate ships and islands. The children have two different-sized vegetable boxes. One of the mathematical intentions of telling the story the adult had was about capacity. First, about the smaller box:

'Oh! He fits in there, if you squeeze him in. Maybe', says Corey.
'Little animals go underneath and big animals go on top', says Olivia. 'The little ones go underneath, the little ones go underneath, and the big ones go on top.'
'She's asking if she can fit in?' says Corey with a mooing cow in his hand.
'Only the little one can come in', confirms Olivia.
Then about the larger vegetable box:
'Those big ones go in here with the bear', replies Olivia.
'Only, if they can all fit in', Corey reaffirms.

Children as mathematical narrative authors in play

I observe Jake play with story-related materials following the 'Ladybird on a Leaf' story (Figure 3.1). The mathematical idea of this storytelling was that a number, say 'N', always remains unchanged if the number added and then subtracted from it is the same or the number remains unchanged if the number subtracted and then added to it is the same. Haylock and Cockburn offer a specific example from which a generalisation can be made: 'If you add 6 to a number and then subtract 6 from the answer you always get back to the number you started with' (2013, p.297). The story below allows us to play with these mathematical ideas, which can be represented as: $N + n - n = N$ and $N - n + n = N$.

Jake listens to this story and afterwards chooses a ladybird; after an interesting discussion with another child about how ladybirds can probably have different numbers of spots, he decides to play with 12 spots. Jake carefully arranges these as a six and a six on each wing. The ladybird and spots are cut out from sugar paper. Following on from this is a mathematical observation of Jake playing with story-related props and retelling the story (Figure 3.2) (his words are in italic).

'Ladybird on a Leaf' (Jake listens to this story)

Once upon a leaf there was a ladybird. She was enjoying the warm sun on her wings. 'Good for my spots', she thought as she turned around to catch the rays. From her leaf she could see many ladybirds doing just the same. She was disappointed that she was not the only one. At least her spots were arranged in a way that pleased her: a lovely pattern making ten. Ten black spots, not nine, not eight, not seven, not six, not five, not four, not three, not two, not one, but ten beautifully arranged spots. She closed her eyes and went into a sort of lonely doze.

Just then her telephone rang. She slid it out from between her wings. 'Yes?' she asked, wondering who could be calling at this time. Her phone never rang these days. She had lost contact with most ladybirds.
'Hello. It's me, Camilla. Where are you? What are you doing? Would you like to go to London?'
'Too many questions,' thought the ladybird as she held the phone further away from her ear, so that she could think. 'Camilla. Camilla. Camilla. Oh yeah! Camilla.' She had not seen her in years. Donkey's years (whatever that means, she thought to herself).
'Would you like to go to London?'
'When?' the ladybird asked.
'Today', came the reply. 'I'll be with you soon.'

The ladybird started to dust down the leaf and generally fuss about. She thought no one knew about her secret: her spots were artificial and wash off in heavy rain; but an ant from the leaf above had seen her glue spots on each day. Camilla was often early, so the ladybird needed to be ready and not caught out sticking on spots. There was a mischievous rain cloud above her leaf, who wanted to upset her prized look. He washed two spots off and said:

'What's gone is gone.'
The friendly ant above noticed this. He dipped into the spot glue and added the two spots back on to the ladybird's back.
The ant whispered, 'what's on is on'.
The ant went back to his breakfast. The rain cloud washed four spots off.
'What's gone is gone', the rain cloud hissed.
The ant returned, only slightly irritated with being disturbed again. He replaced the four spots and looked up at the rain cloud.
'What's on is on', the ant whispered.
The doorbell rang and Camilla commented on how well the ladybird looked with her perfect ten spots.
'Time flies. Now hurry we need to catch the train to ladybird London,' said Camilla.

Figure 3.1 Jake playing with 'Ladybird on a Leaf' story-related props to create the pattern
12 − n + n = 12.

Jake (4 years and 5 months) plays with the 'Ladybird on a Leaf'

mathematical idea N − n + n = N

or

12 − n + n = 12 as Jake chooses 12 spots for his ladybird

Jake works through the following mathematical ideas

12 − 4 + 4 = 12

12 − 7 + 7 = 12

12 − 12 + 12 = 12

12 − 10 + 10 = 12

Jake's play

What strikes me as I transcribe a video recording of Jake is how he carefully threads mathematical ideas through his play. He brushes off the spots from the ladybird, and talks through number relationships for 12. There is immediacy to this: he doesn't think first about the number relationship, then remove the spots. His actions are the possibility question 'what if?' as he doesn't know what the outcome of removing 7 from 12 is. He expresses ideas of the original story heard, i.e. you start with a number 'N' then subtract a number 'n' then replace the same number 'n', to arrive back to the original number 'N'. Jake uses the ladybird body and spots to represent this abstract idea in visual, physical and verbal ways.

Capturing Jake's mathematical behaviour

In Chapter 1 I set out an observational tool to record children's mathematical behaviour. Through the theoretical discussion in this chapter play is seen as mathematical in the way children pose and solve problems. Alongside the narrative description it is useful to filter out Jake's playful mathematical behaviour. By placing this descriptive account alongside ideas concerning mathematics, an observation of a child's mathematical behaviour is achieved. Connections between the labels on the left and the description can be made visual using arrows or highlighting. This record can be a catalyst for discussion with children and other adults including parents (Carr 2001).

The landscape observation of Jake maps with arrows some connections between what Jake expresses and theoretical ideas about mathematics. It is more manageable to pick up on some rather than all possible connections. I recommend that observational accounts are supported with audio recordings of children and it is worth referring to the work of Paley (1999; 1981) to discover the value of recording children's stories and dramatisations.

Jake represents the pattern $N - n + n = N$ through four of his own number relationship patterns. He uses addition and subtraction to work out what the number relationships are. Jake's action of removing spots is a physical conjectural question: what if I remove seven spots? He needs to check the number of spots removed asking 'what is three more than four?' before working through what seven is in relation to 12.

Jake transfers the mathematical idea at the heart of the 'Ladybird on a Leaf' story to a play context. He uses story language to support expression of mathematical ideas: 'The sneaky rain takes spots away and the ant adds spots back on', articulating mathematical ideas in imaginative ways.

Play is unpredictable

Children operate in specialised ways in play: sometimes creating oral mathematical narrative. It must be noted that mathematical expression in play narrative is very

Mathematical observation Jake

Mathematical feature	Narrative description 'Ladybird on a Leaf'
Conjecturing: 'What if?' (problem posing)	*The sneaky rain took four away.* *Soon the sun came along, the sun came along and put four back.* [Jake replaces two spots on each wing.] *The ladybird thanks the sun for making the spots come back.*
Algorithm (for example, adding, subtracting, multiplying, dividing)	*This time the sneaky rain took more than four away. She, the sneaky rain takes two away.* [Jakes hands are over the spots one hand each over two spots on either wing.] *She decided to take more than two, more than four.* *She decided to take three more than four. Three more makes ... Hey, how many does it makes? 1, 2, 3, 4, 5, 6, 7.* *She took seven away. The rain took seven away. She only had five spots left.* *Soon she called for her friend the little ant* [Jake starts replacing spots] *she puts on 1, 2, 3* [placing three spots on one wing], *4, 5, 6, 7.*
Mathematical utterances (mathematical words)	Jake places four spots on the other wing. The spot arrangement is restored to six on each wing.] *Where did my other ones go?* [Jake asks looking around.] *'1, 2, 3, 4, 5, 6, 7, 8, 9, 10, 11, 12 ... there is 12 actually.'* [Jake counts and touches each spot saying the number names.]
Mathematical facts	*The ant went away to have some tea and cake* [Jake shows motion of an ant walking off with his fingers.] Then he uses both hands to brush off six spots from each wing. She says [difficult to hear but something about the ladybird having no spots. He holds the sugar paper ladybird vertically.] *Soon she cries 'help' and the ant says, 'what now?'*
Generalisation (making mathematical connections seeing patterns)	*She says all my spots are washed away.* *And soon the ladybird, the ant, put 1, 2, 3, 4, 5, 6 ...* [Jake starts arranging spots over two wings but changes this to placing six on one wing before starting on the other]. *7, 8, 9, 10, 11, 12. She putted 12 more on.*
Mathematical mistakes or misunderstandings	[Jake pushes the spots further up the ladybird body.] *And soon she thanked the ant. And soon ... the rain washed this many away ...*
Transferring mathematical ideas to play contexts	[There are two spots left. Jake starts to count the spots on the carpet.] *1, 2, 3, 4, 5, 6, 7, 8, 9 ... nine away.* *And soon the ant came along and the ant was quite cross and soon the ant said 'I was just about to have my tea and cake.'*
Curiosity (within mathematical context)	*And soon the sun sawed the naughty rain trying to get the spots away and soon the sun was so cross and said* *'Go away naughty rain, go away'*
Fluency (ease of use of mathematical ideas)	[Jake replaces six spots on each wing, restoring the original twelve to how he started.]

Figure 3.2 Completed observational tool

Title	Age of child in years and months	Gender	Context	Initials of observer	Date	Audio recorded reference
'Ladybird on a leaf'	4 years 5 months	Male	Playing with related props following adult storytelling	CMcG	26.4.2013	DM650000

Prompts	Observer comments
Transfer of mathematical ideas to context such as play or retelling stories	Jake retelling 'Ladybird on a Leaf' Mathematical idea N−n+n=N or 12−n+n=12 Prior to the narrative account Jake makes a careful choice of 12 spots for his ladybird following a discussion with another child where he concludes that ladybirds can have however many spots they wish. Jake plays with the sugar paper ladybird and spots in a way that transfers the story and mathematical ideas of a story told by an adult to a play situation. What is interesting and not obvious from this record is how other children are listening to Jake, while playing with their mini ladybirds.
Use of props	Jake uses the props thoughtfully in a way that supports his actions. He uses the spots to work out how many he has taken away and how many are left. He works through number relationships using the props: 12−4=8; 12−7=5;12−12=0; 12−10=−2. These sequences relate to the original story of N−n+n=N; 12−4=8+4=12 or 12−4+4=12; 12−7=5+7=12 or 12−7+7=12; 12−12=0+12=12 or 12−12+12=12. He intends 12−10=2+10=12 or 12−10+10=12 but makes an error and thinks there are 9 rather than 10. Jake starts with 12 spots and repeats the pattern of removing a number and adding back on the same number, four times. Jake retells the story in a way that preserves the original mathematical idea of the story told.
Connection to original story heard	There are close parallels between Jake's story and that of the story heard. It is worth noting how Jake extends the mathematical idea of number complements to a number of his choice and how this number challenges his thinking.
Extending ideas	There is a teaching opportunity to draw out more of the possibilities for the mathematical story pattern for 12 (12−n+n=12) using different numbers for n. This could help Jake become fluent with other number complements for 12.
Follow up	It would be good to show the video or listen to the audio recording with Jake and his parent(s). Jake is acquiring English as a Second Language and this observation tells us something of his ability to use story language to express mathematical ideas. The recording of Jake playing and retelling the story can be shared along with a copy of this documented account with Jake, his parent(s) and staff.

Outcome of discussion with child	Outcome of discussion with parent
Jake's comment on watching the DVD of himself retelling 'Ladybird on a Leaf': 'Hey Mum, not only 6+6 makes 12 spots! 5+7 and 4+8 also make 12!'	Jake's mother writes the following comment on watching the DVD recording of Jake retelling "Ladybird on a Leaf': 'He noticed that there could be several combinations of numbers to make the same total' and 'we are very pleased to see Jake enjoying himself in this project. It seems that this creative approach of using ladybird spots really has got Jake interested and has made him think mathematically in relation to the story.'

Figure 3.2 Continued

unpredictable: children's play is not predetermined by children or adults. Play narrative tells the story of children's ideas: play narrative can be 'mathematical narrative' (Pound & Lee 2011). It is important to realise that we cannot as adults force this agenda. On many occasions I observe children following a story with mathematical emphasis and their play takes unrelated directions. Play scenarios may be rich in problem posing and solving but are not always an expression of specific story ideas.

Conclusion

If as an adult you allow a child to lead you in play, you sense how children thread imaginative ideas through play, and how there is something very immediate about this threading. Thoughts, actions and words work together to form ideas, which, like the antennae of an insect, search out new direction. Ideas dominate as objects take on newly agreed meanings: in 'Play for Tomorrow' (1991) children agree that a toilet roll holder is a telescope, which supports the opening quote to this chapter: 'In play thought is separated from objects and action arises from ideas rather than from things: a piece of wood begins to be a doll and a stick becomes a horse' (Vygotsky, 1978, p.97).

Play, mathematics and story are difficult to define in ways that fully encompass what they are about; ideas about play, mathematics and story bind them together. Problem posing and solving are common to story, mathematics and play. Children are authors of their play narratives, using props and materials to express abstract thought in a purposeful way.

Children's play is mathematical as they pose and solve problems; as they symbolise ideas; as they express abstract ideas. Defining play through the lens of problem posing and problem solving helps us to see how mathematical play is. Observations of play following the 'Teremok' and 'Ladybird on a Leaf' stories show children expressing mathematical ideas in explicit ways. Corey and Olivia play with soft animal toys and vegetable boxes, expressing positional language. Jake plays with the cut-out ladybird and 12 spots in a purposeful way. He physically, verbally and visually expresses mathematical ideas. Jake takes the mathematical idea of the original story N–n+n=N, testing number relationships for 12 in this play context. This is an example of transferring mathematical ideas from story to play in a precise way. In this play scenario, Jake's actions, thoughts and words work together in a slow turning kaleidoscopic way.

Children are authors of their play narratives, using props and materials to express abstract ideas in a purposeful play way. Children author their own play narrative, which can be a mathematical narrative (Pound & Lee 2011), though not always. Play is implicitly about problem posing and problem solving: play sometimes expresses explicit mathematical ideas.

Picture books

Meaningful mathematical contexts

Contemporary picture books bend, stretch, or break the rules, and in this play with conventions, a space between the 'real' world and other possible worlds is opened up.

(Haynes & Murris 2012, p.39)

This chapter aims to explore:

- children's literature as a pedagogical choice to support mathematics
- relationships between story and mathematics in picture books
- learning-supportive characteristics of picture books.

'The Doorbell Rang'

Ma makes 12 cookies and gives them to Victoria and Sam; six cookies each. The doorbell rings and is opened to two children. Twelve cookies shared between four children gives three cookies each. The doorbell rings and is opened to two more children. Twelve cookies shared between six children gives two cookies each. The doorbell rings and is opened to six children. Twelve cookies shared between twelve children gives one cookie each. The doorbell rings. Ma suggests the children eat the cookies before it is opened. Sam looks through the letter box and the door opens to Grandma with a tray of cookies. The doorbell rings again.

(Hutchins 1986)

Introduction

This chapter is about finding mathematical opportunity in picture books. There are three strands to this chapter: first, acknowledging that picture books, storybooks and traditional nursery rhymes are ways of children experiencing mathematical ideas. Mathematical ideas are often contextualised in a meaningful way in story contexts (Hong 1996; Schiro 2004; Welchman-Tischler 1992; Van den Heuvel-Panhuizen and Van den Boogaard 2008): a character such as Mouse has a problem to solve: he needs to put together a construction kit, to make an aeroplane so that he can travel to Rat's house, which requires problem solving strategies (see Chapter 1).

Second, we are interested in seeing how story and mathematics work together in such ways that one does not overpower the other. In the case of 'No Problem!' there is harmony between a simple story and ideas of problem solving. Brown (2013c) shares her concern that some 'mathematical stories' are forced, fabricated or stylised, that something is lost in using these stories to teach mathematics. There needs to be harmony between story and mathematics if the experience is to be genuine.

The third strand of this chapter is to tease out the supportive mathematical learning characteristics that picture books can have (Van den Heuvel-Panhuizen & Elia 2012). Our understanding of these learning characteristics may influence our choice of picture book as well as focusing our minds on mathematical opportunities they present.

Questions:

What is the range of mathematical possibilities in a picture book?

How do story and mathematics relate?

What would we look for in a picture book to support mathematics?

Children's literature as a pedagogical choice to support mathematics

Picture books, storybooks and nursery rhymes are sources of mathematical ideas. Well-written published stories often have mathematical ideas at their core. Picture books of high literacy value, books in which the author simply wants to tell children a fascinating story and are not written with the intention of teaching children mathematical concepts, often have the potential to evoke thinking about mathematics (Van den Heuvel-Panhuizen & Van den Boogaard 2008). Picture books contextualise mathematical ideas in meaningful ways for children, wrapping emotional and cognitive engagement together (Hong 1996). Mathematical ideas of stories may be accidental,

Number stories in picture books

Susie Weaver, a headteacher with a passion for story as a way of teaching mathematics, inspires trainee early-years practitioners every year when she presents to Early Childhood Studies foundation degree students about Number Stories. There is a hush in the room as students turn the pages of picture books and represent mathematics they find as number stories, on blank pieces of paper. Students realise rich mathematical opportunity in stories such as 'The Giant Jam Sandwich' (Lord & Burroway 1972), 'The Greedy Triangle' (Burns 1994) and 'The Doorbell Rang' (Hutchins 1986). Susie invites students to look at the work of children who have represented the mathematics of these stories. Trainee educators are surprised by the mathematical opportunities in these picture books.

(Weaver 2013)

part of the story fabric, a consequence of story ideas (Browne 2013; Burroway 2009). These mathematical ideas need teasing out so that as adults we understand how they fit as part of story structure and how they can be played with to prompt mathematical ideas, which I do through analysis of 'The Doorbell Rang' later in this chapter.

Meaningful mathematical engagement through picture books

Children who learn well are engaged. Engagement is about how student and instructional content interact (Van den Heuvel-Panhuizen & Van den Boogaard 2008). Keat and Wilburne (2009) describe how successful learners are enthusiastic and show interest, curiosity, pleasure and motivation. Keat and Wilburne (2009) associate 'engagement' with the words attention, flexibility, persistence and self-regulation to the learning process. As educators we look for ways to enthuse, to engage the children we teach, and one of the joys of teaching young children is that they are naturally enthusiastic learners, responding positively to story.

Mathematical engagement and achievement

Research with particular focus on how children's literature positively influences children's mathematical engagement and achievement is discussed as follows.

Van den Heuvel-Panhuizen and Van den Boogaard (2008) find that their chosen picture book *Vijfde zijn* ('Being Fifth') has the power to elicit mathematics-related thinking. Their research closely analyses mathematical utterances of children who are reading a picture book. Mathematical engagement is evident even when there is no instructional purpose, the book has not been written with the intention of teaching mathematics and the content does not explicitly display mathematics. The book creates an environment in which children construct mathematical knowledge in meaningful ways. They conclude that a picture book can tell a compelling story and unintentionally provides contexts for mathematical thinking (Van den Heuvel-Panhuizen & Van den Boogaard 2008).

Hong (1996) highlights how children's literature has in the past supported social and emotional development along with linguistic abilities. Hong's (1996) research explores the effectiveness of teaching mathematics through children's literature in terms of improving both the disposition to pursue mathematical learning and the achievement of mathematical learning. Hong's (1996) study involves 57 Korean kindergarten children who are divided into two groups. One group, which Hong calls the experimental group, listens to maths-related stories and plays with maths materials related to storybook content: children listen to 'Goldilocks and the Three Bears' and play with shoes, shirts and hats, ordering these from large to small. The other group of children experience ordinary storybook and maths materials unrelated to story context.

Hong (1996) finds that children's literature with mathematically related ideas can act as a catalyst to motivate children because it provides meaningful contexts for mathematical ideas. If children are given activities, such as the ordering activity following 'Goldilocks and the Three Bears', they apply themselves to mathematical work for longer and become deeply involved in the learning.

Keat and Wilburne (2009) researched how storybooks influence achievement and positive approaches to learning mathematics. Outcomes of this work describe how 'the children were constructing mathematical knowledge and honing mathematical skills in ways that assured both achievement and positive attitudes and approaches to learning mathematics' (Keat & Wilburne 2009). Construction of mathematical knowledge came about because the characters of story allow for playful learning opportunities (Keat & Wilburne 2009). Hong (1996) finds that children's disposition to voluntarily pursue mathematical learning increases using children's literature. These research findings support the use of children's literature to engage children with mathematics.

Story catalysts

Engagement with a picture book is evident in the following example resulting from working with children on the oral mathematical story project. Children aged four and five listen to an oral telling of 'My Cat Likes to Hide in Boxes' (Dodd & Sutton 1978), then voluntarily pursue mathematical ideas as they make boxes for cats to hide in.

The picture book 'My Cat Likes to Hide in Boxes' is catalytic to this child's mathematical motivation (see Figure 4.1). A child's decision to make boxes for cats as flattened 'net' constructions is sophisticated mathematical thinking. Storybooks can act as a catalyst to motivate children and provide interesting and engaging contexts (Hong 1996). Connecting literature to play through story-related materials offers children a way to work through story associated mathematical ideas.

'My Cat Likes to Hide in Boxes'

Suzanne, a Reception class teacher, describes how following a telling of the story 'My Cat Likes to Hide in Boxes' children work with Polydron to make boxes for cats to hide in. It can be difficult to get Polydron pieces to fit together, and Rita decides to find a way around this by putting them together as a flat structure before folding them up (creating a net). Children engage with this box making activity for 45 minutes, which is much longer than expected for these children aged four or five.

(Kelham 2013a)

Figure 4.1 A child using Polydron to make a box for a cat after listening to the story 'My Cat Likes to Hide in Boxes'.

Story-related play

As well as the ordering activity, Hong (1996) offers children other tasks, one of which uses three number components to make a number e.g. 8=3+2+3. Hong (1996) observes that 'more of the experimental group of children use numbers greater than 10 in their number combination tasks', which connects to an observation I make as part of the oral mathematical story project where Jake chooses 12 rather than 10 spots to create his own number complements as he retells 'Ladybird on a Leaf'. Jake shows a disposition to pursue more challenging mathematical ideas than those he hears in the story.

'Ladybird on a Leaf'

In Chapter 3, Jake chooses a larger number (12) than that of the story he hears (10) and his own number relationships (e.g. 12 – 7 = 5) as he plays with story-related materials in a deep thinking way. Jake's play is related to the story but he applies the story idea to his own mathematical idea. A story context offers Jake opportunity for deep thinking.

Children's literature offers possibilities for integrating mathematics with literacy in a positive way. Hong (1996) argues that narrative forms of knowing support memory, and that stories provide problems in a narrative context. Hong (1996) states that 'the use of storybooks can thus be a relevant way to expose mathematical concepts to children because stories provide children with problem situations and solutions in a narrative context', which is the case with sharing of cookies in 'The Doorbell Rang'. The narrative context of this story connects mathematical ideas of addition and division in a meaningful way.

Children's literature can be used to:

provide meaningful contexts
introduce story-related materials
offer creative mathematical experiences
pose interesting problems
develop a mathematical concept or skill
demonstrate use of mathematics
introduce vocabulary associated with mathematics.

(Based on Hong 1996)

Educational implications

Research findings that support the use of children's literature for improving the disposition to pursue mathematical learning and mathematical thinking (Hong 1996; Keat & Wilburne 2009; Van den Heuvel-Panhuizen & Van den Boogaard 2008) have educational implications. This pedagogical approach assists integration of curricula: mathematics, literacy and social skills connect through story characters (Hong 1996; Keat & Wilburne 2009). As well as integrating curricula story holds the following educational implications:

- Picture books have the power to evoke mathematical thinking (Van den Heuvel-Panhuizen & Van den Boogaard 2008).
- The use of literature to support mathematics allows practice using mathematical language (Keat & Wilburne 2009).
- Story characters offer playful learning opportunities, which is central to children's development (Vygotsky 1978).
- A story can be reread or retold several times to support learning (Keat & Wilburne 2009).

Relationships between story and mathematics in picture books

How do mathematical ideas and imaginative ideas connect in picture books? Dismantling a picture book shows how story and mathematics work together. 'The Doorbell Rang' by Pat Hutchins is a good example of a well-written picture book where story and mathematics work together in unintentional but harmonious ways.

'The Doorbell Rang' by Pat Hutchins

Analysis of 'The Doorbell Rang' provides two insights. First, we see how place, character and plot work together to form a story. Second, this analysis makes explicit how some stories are rich with mathematical possibilities. The story is based on a simple idea. Cookies are presented to two children, but then the doorbell rings, which means the cookies need to be shared and so reduce in number. The doorbell rings and each time the cookie share changes. When the share reduces to one cookie it is suggested by an adult that the door is not opened. Sam is rewarded for his decision to override this suggestion when he opens the door to his grandmother, who has a tray of cookies.

In this picture book there is scope to explore number relationships for 12 as it is divided by two to give six; by four to give three; by six to give two; by 12 to give one with each doorbell ring.

Story of the cookies:

12 cookies divided by 2 children = 6 cookies
12 cookies divided by 4 children = 3 cookies
12 cookies divided by 6 children = 2 cookies
12 cookies divided by 12 children = 1 cookie

There is another mathematical idea threading through this story: to start there are two children in the kitchen but more arrive in a pattern.
Story of the children:

2 children
2 children and 2 children = 4 children
2 children and 2 children and 2 children = 6 children
2 children and 2 children and 2 children and 6 children = 12 children

More and more children arrive until there are 12 around the kitchen table. There is, as it were, a mathematical story of addition as two children, two more children, and six children are added to the starting two, within a story of division where 12 is divided by a pattern of 2, 4, 6, and 12. Behind the simplicity of a repeated sequence of doorbell ringing lies complexity that glues the story together. These number relationships work together behind the scenes. There is an addition story within a division story, within a story about the need to share as each doorbell ring brings more children.

Playing with the plot to prompt mathematical ideas

If we focus on number relationships between 12, four and three we can play between using either four or three as a denominator. Twelve cookies divided by four children is three cookies each: 12 cookies divided by three children is four cookies each. The 12 divided by three number relationship is not part of the picture book story. If we choose to retell the story with emphasis on 12 divided by three, relationships between 12, 4 and 3 can be made explicit. To do this we will need to change something about the story, maybe having children arriving in ones:

12 cookies divided by 3 children = 4 cookies
12 cookies divided by 4 children = 3 cookies

The story can be retold with this small change. Victoria and Sam have a plate of 12 cookies; the doorbell rings and it is Tom from next door. The 12 cookies need to be divided between three children to give four each. This playfulness with the plot can draw out the relationship between 12 cookies and three children. This is the value of moving to oral storytelling: playfulness with the plot.

This story separated into its finer parts discovers two number operations i.e. addition and division working together in harmony. Arrival of children represents an important pattern as these are the denominators for the cookies, which stay fixed as a numerator, 12. Factors of 12 (2, 6); (4, 3); (6, 2); (12, 1) feature as part of the story and become apparent as the denominator (number of children) changes from 2 to 4 to 6 to 12.

Story of children and cookies:

12 cookies divided by 2 children = 6 cookies
12 cookies divided by 3 children = 4 cookies
12 cookies divided by 4 children = 3 cookies
12 cookies divided by 6 children = 2 cookies
12 cookies divided by 12 children = 1 cookie

Story language

The story language is mathematical: children listen to phrases, 'that's six each'; 'that's three each'; 'that's two each'; 'that's one each'. The story articulates number relationships with the worrying sense that beyond 12 there will be a disappointment as with the next doorbell ring, one biscuit could diminish, and who wants less than a whole biscuit? Children listening to the story see addition with each doorbell ring, division with each invitation of 'you can share the cookies'. Story and mathematical ideas work together: addition and division work together in meaningful ways with the story idea of a doorbell ringing for unexpected visitors.

Simple ideas working together in complex ways

As educators we could easily be deceived by the simplicity of this story and miss the opportunity for mathematics. Unless we take this story apart we could miss the mathematical possibilities. By setting out separate pieces (like Shrew in 'No Problem!') we appreciate the opportunity of using addition alongside division in the context of sharing the cookies.

What starts out as a simple idea develops into a complex network of ideas. This story supports the principle of helping children make connections between mathematical ideas (Haylock & Cockburn 2013). We start to think of other patterns and possibilities by asking ourselves 'what if?' questions. What if different numbers of children arrive, three instead of four? What if some children have to leave when the doorbell rings? We can play with the story to prompt other connections: if eight children were to share the 12 cookies, how would this work? By disrupting relationships between story and mathematics we open out other mathematical opportunities. 'The Doorbell Rang' shows story and mathematics working together in surprisingly simple and yet complex ways.

Learning-supportive characteristics of picture books

Van den Heuvel-Panhuizen and Elia (2012) devise what they call learning-supportive characteristics of a picture book. These learning characteristics sharpen our mind to choices of picture books that support mathematical learning, and highlight the mathematical learning possibilities of picture books. The learning-supportive characteristics are summarised as follows.

Relevance:

    contains valuable mathematical content
    mathematics is presented in a meaningful context

Degree of connection:

    connects with children's life and world
    connects mathematics with interests of children
    connects mathematics and reality
    shows coherence within mathematics
    establishes relationships with other subjects

Scope:

    makes understanding possible at different levels
    offers multiple layers of meaning
    anticipates future concept development

Participation opportunities:

    offers children opportunities for involvement
    engages children cognitively/emotionally/physically.

                       (Van den Heuvel-Panhuizen & Elia 2012)

The degree of connection is what makes the ideas meaningful for a child. Hughes finds that children offer a different response when the nature of the question or task is made meaningful, advising: 'young children were frequently more competent than Piaget had maintained, particularly if they were studied in contexts that made sense to them such as when playing simple games' (1986, p.viii). Story gives children a context for mathematical ideas.

Against the learning-supportive characteristics we place the illustrated story 'The Doorbell Rang' (Hutchins 1996).

Relevance:

Contains valuable mathematical content: division is a mathematical idea concerning sharing of cookies. Addition is a way of establishing the increasing number of children or denominator.

Mathematics is presented in a meaningful context: children relate to the possibility of the number of cookies reducing as there are more children to share with and fewer cookies to enjoy.

Degree of connection:

Connects with children's life and world: sharing is an important aspect of children's emotional, and social development.

Connects mathematics with interests of children: sharing out is a relevant application of division.

Connects mathematics and reality: dividing is a mathematical idea children encounter in everyday life.

Shows coherence within mathematics: addition and division work together in a coherent way. The doorbell ringing brings more children, which need to be added so that the cookies can be shared. There are two mathematical procedures working together in a connected way: addition and division.

Establishes relationships with other subjects: literacy, mathematics and social skills connect through the story ideas of sharing.

Scope:

Makes understanding possible at different levels: on one level cookies are shared; on more complex levels number relationships between addition and division work together.

Offers multiple layers of meaning: mathematical content operates through many layers, depending on how one tunes in to this. Picture illustrations make the division visual.

Anticipates future concept development: children can take this thinking forward to play opportunities with story-related props. Number relationships can be further explored; there is potential to look at sharing 12 cookies between four children and between three children, drawing out the idea that if 12 cookies are divided by four children there will be three cookies and then, moving out from the story as it is, if 12 cookies are divided by three children there will be four cookies.

Participation opportunities:

Offers children opportunities for involvement: children can provide the repeated phrase, 'No one makes cookies like Grandma'.

Engages children cognitively/emotionally/physically: children can play with story-related props before, during or after the story is read or retold. Play-related opportunity brings physical involvement.

Learning characteristic: stories make understanding possible at different levels

The learning-supportive characteristic that 'makes understanding possible at different levels' (Van den Heuvel-Panhuizen & Elia 2012) relates well to the example of 'The Doorbell Rang'. On one level, cookies are being shared out; on another level number relationships concerning 12 divided by increasing numbers 2, 4, 6 and 12 are evident. The picture book 'The Doorbell Rang' offers 'multiple layers of meaning' (Van den Heuvel-Panhuizen & Elia 2012) making division ideas accessible for children at different levels.

Conclusion

This chapter shows how picture books are a source of mathematical ideas that contextualise mathematics in meaningful ways for children. This chapter analyses 'The Doorbell Rang' to see relationships between mathematics and story; connections between addition and division and learning-supportive characteristics, all of which highlight the value in using picture books to support mathematical thinking. (A story profile for 'The Doorbell Rang' is set out in Appendix 4.) The nib of a story inks mathematical and story ideas, which flow together. Though the main focus is on picture books, similar analysis can be applied to other forms of children's literature.

A number of research studies (Hong 1996; Keat & Wilburne 2009; Van den Heuvel-Panhuizen & Van den Boogaard 2008) recommend the use of children's picture books to support mathematical learning. Children's literature positively influences disposition to pursue mathematics learning (Hong 1996). Potential relationships between picture books and mathematics are worth exploiting, particularly as evidence indicates children respond favourably to this pedagogical approach. However, these mathematical ideas should remain as part of the story experience, enjoyed by the child (Byrant 1947). The challenge to the storyteller is to preserve these stories.

There are three reasons to examine a picture book; the first is to see how a story is structured; how the components fit together. Second, this analysis allows us to understand the fabric, the tailoring, the pattern of the story; relationships between mathematics and story. Analysis allows us to get to the pockets of the story where mathematics is hidden. The third reason is to see learning-supportive characteristics picture books have to offer (Heuvel-Panhuizen & Elia 2012).

These insights equip us to move between modes of discourse: written to oral; reading to telling. Telling allows even greater flexibility of mathematical thinking as problems are posed by the character of the story, the storyteller or the listening child. This chapter prepares the reader for storytelling in that it spreads out the mathematical pieces of a picture book so that they can be put together to make another construction: an oral mathematical story, which we do in Chapter 5.

Oral mathematical story

Moving from picture books to oral mathematical story

Humpty Dumpty

Humpty Dumpty sat on a wall,
Humpty Dumpty had a great fall:
All the King's horses and all the King's men
Couldn't put Humpty together again.

(Traditional Nursery Rhyme, Matterson 1991)

This chapter aims to:

- find relationships between story and mathematical ideas: story of 'Little Lumpty' and counting in multiples of two to the twelfth multiple
- move from picture books to oral storytelling
- tell the story of what happens when an oral mathematical story is taken to the classroom.

'Little Lumpty'

In the little town of Dumpty there was a high wall. Humpty Dumpty had fallen from it long, long ago. But people still remembered him.
Every day children played by the wall and sang,
'Humpty Dumpty sat on the wall. Humpty Dumpty had a great fall.'
Little Lumpty loved the wall and always dreamed about climbing to the top.
'Don't ever do that', Lumpty's mother said. 'Remember, all the king's horses and all the king's men couldn't put Humpty Dumpty together again.'
But Little Lumpty couldn't stop thinking about the wall. One day, on his way home from school, he found a long ladder and dragged it to the wall.
He climbed up . . . and up . . . and up.

At last he reached the top. 'Oh, there's my house! And there's my school! I can almost touch the clouds!'

Lumpty was so happy that he danced along like a tightrope walker.

'If only my friends could see me now!'

But then Little Lumpty looked down. IT WAS A BIG MISTAKE. His legs began to shake and tremble.

'Oh, no! I don't think I can get back to the ladder.'

'What if I'm not home by dinner time?'

Darkness sets in and Little Lumpty remembers what happened to Humpty Dumpty. He screams for help. The people of the town spread out and hold a blanket, which he bounces on three times. He explains to his mother that he had to see what it was like on top of the wall. Little Lumpty tells the moon of his love of the wall, before falling asleep.

(Imai 1994)

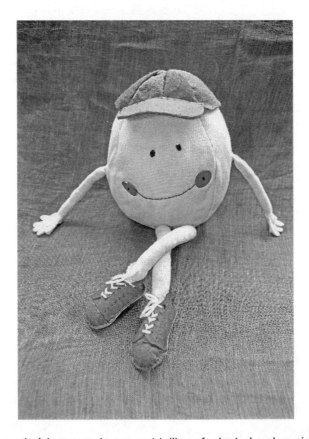

Figure 5.1 Little Lumpty (story prop to support telling of adapted oral version).

Introduction

This chapter aims to describe what happens when oral mathematical story is used as a pedagogical approach with a class of 30 children aged five and six years old. It is intended that these insights will prepare the reader to create oral mathematical story experiences for children.

The nursery rhyme Humpty Dumpty connects to the story 'Little Lumpty' in that Lumpty decides to take on the same challenge as Humpty but survives. A child points out an opportunity to connect the story of Little Lumpty to mathematics: 'You could count the steps of his ladder', an idea that is developed further to counting in multiples of two, each rung of the ladder bringing Little Lumpty up two bricks higher (see Figure 5.2).

In the context of an infant school, with all the classroom complexities such an environment has, I take the role of storyteller and the class teacher takes the role of observer. The teacher captures responses of children that would otherwise go unnoticed. The class teacher is surprised by how some children respond: her normal expectations are disrupted.

To start, I explain to a child of five that I need a story with a mathematical idea, which I can tell from my head.

'Little Lumpty', she suggests with shocking certainty.

'Why?' I probe.

'Because, you can count the steps on the ladder, and the number of people who hold the blanket when Little Lumpty jumps', she replies.

I latch onto two ideas: adapting the story of 'Little Lumpty' from picture book format to an oral story format; and exploring the mathematical possibilities of using the ladder for counting.

Despite this helpful start, the prospect of applying the research idea is fraught with risk: risk of a research idea with the fragility of an egg rolling over the edge and breaking; risk as an educator from a different place (Higher Education) sits in front of 30 children; risk as a personal oral mathematical story creation goes public. I am putting my money where my mouth is!

Relationships between story and mathematical ideas: 'Little Lumpty' and counting in multiples of two to the twelfth multiple

I am drawn to the story of 'Little Lumpty' not only because a child of five sees connections between the fabric of the story and mathematics, but also because of the link with the traditional nursery rhyme Humpty Dumpty. I can use this as a repetitive phrase to hook children in and give me time to think if I forget where to go. If I lose my way, I can probably say these familiar words at the same time as thinking 'where next?'

Mathematical ideas in the picture book can be drawn from the text and from the illustrations:

Mathematical ideas in the story of 'Little Lumpty':

height of wall

historical time 'long, long, ago' and the historical fall of Humpty

time changing over course of a day (dinner time and getting dark)

length of long ladder

positional language 'up; top'

perspective from a distance (looking down from a height) 'down'

distance across top of wall to ladder

size of blanket (big)

stretched (area)

number of people to hold the blanket (4 sides x 3 people on each side = 12 in total).

Mathematical language in the story:

'long'; 'up'; 'top'; 'down'; 'bottom'; 'bounced once, twice, three times'.

A story profile for 'Little Lumpty' is provided in Appendix 5. Mathematical learning-supportive characteristics as proposed by Van den Heuvel-Panhuizen and Elia (2012) can be summarised as follows:

'Little Lumpty' learning-supportive characteristics

Relevance:

Little Lumpty sets himself the challenge of climbing the wall from which Humpty Dumpty had his great fall. Little Lumpty climbs up the wall and becomes frightened. He sweats over the height of the wall, needs rescuing and bounces 'one, twice and three times' on the blanket that 12 townspeople stretch out. Children relate to the story context, which connects to a familiar nursery rhyme.

Degree of connection:

Little Lumpty is warned by his mother not to climb the wall. Sometimes people decide to do things they are told not to. Lumpty's house, town, bedroom connect to a child's world. A child is interested to find out what happens particularly as Humpty Dumpty came to a bad end. Lumpty's fear of not being able to get down from the wall poses a problem. Stretching out a blanket is a solution employed in real life situations to save people.

There is potential to establish coherence with number relationships: counting in ones to steady his nerves as he climbs higher; counting in multiples of twos (there is a relationship between the gap of the ladder rungs, the number of bricks and the height of the wall).

Literacy, mathematics and emotional relationships connect through this story. Relationships with his mother and the wider community are evident as he is saved. Lumpty's mother shows understanding and forgiveness.

Scope:

There is scope to tune in to the overall sense of Little Lumpty creating a problem for himself and for others to solve it. There is scope to adapt the story to count in multiples of a number, for example two, three, five, establishing the pattern of the count number.

Mathematical ideas can extend to multiplication by looking at the area of the wall rather than height. If he is to find the area of the wall he could use multiplication language: 'One lot of three is three, two lots of three is six', thinking of multiplication as repeated addition. He is adding the number of bricks in each row to find the total number of bricks to build the wall.

The mathematics can be layered: problem posing and problem solving; counting in multiples of ones, twos or another number to find the height of the wall; multiplication to find the area of the wall.

Participation opportunities:

Children want to find out what happens. Illustrations remind children about Humpty Dumpty breaking! There is the possibility that Lumpty will not return safely home. Children worry for Lumpty because they know this possible outcome.

Imaginary story suggestions can be made as to how Lumpty climbs the wall. Children can join in with the forward and reverse counting pattern to help Lumpty steady his nerves. They can silently mime the missed out number when counting in multiples of twos: one (mime); two (say aloud); three (mime); four (say aloud); five (mime); six (say aloud) and so on, an idea suggested by the class teacher, Lucy Walshe.

Number pattern

Mental strategies based on imaginative mathematical images of story words and props develop confidence in manipulating numbers and articulating patterns. Counting in multiples of a number establishes a number pattern and 'central to our understanding of number relationships is the notion of *pattern*' (Haylock & Cockburn 2013, p.139, italic in original). I am interested in developing the story of 'Little Lumpty' in a way that expresses the number pattern of counting in multiples of a number.

Linking the width between ladder rungs to bricks

The relationship between the gap in the rungs of Lumpty's ladder and the equivalent number of bricks of the wall can be played with. We can use this relationship to count single bricks or to count in multiples and calculate how many bricks high the wall is.

As part of this story I construct a mental image where Lumpty selects a ladder with 12 rungs, each interval between the rungs being equal to two bricks of the wall, and the ladder hooks onto the top of the wall. When Lumpty climbs up the ladder he counts: 2, 4, 6, 8, 10, 12, 14, 16, 18, 20, 22, 24, until he gets to the top. The wall is 24 bricks high. Coming down is hard and to steady his nerves he counts back in twos: 24, 22, 20, 18, 16, 14, 12, 10, 8, 6, 4, 2, and arrives safely on the ground. On telling the story it does not work to refer to zero, as on the ground he is in line with the first brick.

I set about writing out the story with the intention of preserving harmony between story and mathematics. Writing the story out helps connect the story and the mathematical ideas in my mind.

But Little Lumpty couldn't stop thinking about the wall.

One day, on his way home from school, he
found a long ladder and dragged it to the wall.

He climbed up ...
and up ... and up.

Figure 5.2 Little Lumpty climbs the wall and the gap between the rungs of his ladder is
equivalent to two bricks. Copyright © 1994 Miko Imai. From 'Little Lumpty' by
Miko Imai. Reproduced with permission of Walker Books Ltd, London SE11 5HJ
www.walker.co.uk

Retelling of the story with the mathematical intention: 'Counting in multiples of two up to 24'

In the town where Humpty Dumpty fell, lives Little Lumpty. The children of
the town sing the traditional nursery rhyme: 'Humpty Dumpty sat on a wall,
Humpty Dumpty had a great fall, all the King's horses and all the King's men,
couldn't put Humpty together again.'

Little Lumpty gets an idea into his head. He wants to climb the wall and
see what the town of Dumpty is like from the top of the wall. He secretly
searches out a suitable ladder, looking in garden sheds. He finds one he
likes the look of. He sees that each gap between the rungs of the ladder is
roughly the same as two bricks of the wall and that the ladder is 12 rungs
long. He thinks he can manage to carry this hooked ladder over his shoulder.

When the rest of the town is asleep he creeps out into the night, takes this ladder from a nearby shed and hooshes it up to hook to the top of the wall. To steady his nerves he counts in twos: 2, 4, 6, 8, 10, 12, 14, 16, 18, 20, 22 and 24. 'Wow', he says aloud, 'the wall is 24 bricks high'. He pulls himself up and sits on top of the wall and looks at the moon, the stars and the sleeping town. He turns around and looks over the other side of the wall. He sees animals asleep and the hills. He turns back around looking down on the town of Dumpty. Suddenly he becomes frightened, cold and hungry.

He moves back along the wall to the ladder. He knows he must come down now on his own. He counts down in twos until the last rung brings him safely to the ground: 24, 22, 20, 18, 16, 14, 12, 10, 8, 6, 4, 2. He brings the ladder back to the shed like a burglar in the thick of the night. He gets back into bed.

He won't tell anyone that he's been where Humpty Dumpty's been. He wonders if Humpty looked over the other side of the wall before his fall. He is pleased he knows the height of the wall in case he wants to build a wall in another town. He dreams of the pattern of the bricks in the wall: 'Short, long; long, short; short, long . . .'

Before taking the oral mathematical story of 'Little Lumpty' to the classroom I think through the mathematical possibilities and decide on a mathematical theme to follow. After a discussion with the class teacher I settle on counting in multiples of twos to the twelfth multiple. I am deliberately extending the count beyond the tenth multiple, which would bring me to 20, because I am interested in making a connection to a multiplication pattern that includes multiplying two by 12. I intentionally open out a future link between repeated addition and multiplication as well as extending the pattern for some children.

Moving from picture books to oral storytelling

Steps I suggest when moving from a picture story or other published story to oral story are as follows.

1 Select a suitable story and read it. It is important to have a positive feeling about the story. Brown (2013c) tells me about a time when part way through telling a story she realises she doesn't like the story and how important her relationship with a story is. When selecting a story it is good to sketch out mathematical possibilities. It is interesting to invite children's ideas at this stage. You then mull these mathematical connections over and think how they can

be developed: counting in ones, counting in multiples forwards and backwards, multiplication . . . a network of connections starts to form.

2 Write out the story: a way of connecting with the story is to write or type out the story as it is (Corbett 2006). This serves to set the sequence of the story in your mind. This writing out prompts you to adapt it if necessary, editing out unnecessary detail/expanding (Bryant 1947). It may be that you decide some of the content can be removed or that something needs emphasising. In the case of adapting 'Little Lumpty' it is necessary that I place emphasis on his selection of a suitable ladder and the relationship between the gaps between the ladder rungs and number of bricks of the wall. I also adapt the story so that he comes down the ladder and doesn't call for help. He counts backwards in twos to steady his nerves. The story is rewritten in a way that includes these mathematical ideas: counting in twos forwards and backwards.

3 One of the commonly shared fears is how to recall the story. To overcome this I recommend a definite decision about the opening line (once these words are uttered you fall over the edge and abseil down). Story maps (Corbett 2007; 2006; Talk for writing 2008) can be used as a tool to internalise the sequence and made available when retelling the story. Another approach is to divide a page into sections and put a key word, image or some representation in each box for each stage of the story. You may decide on associated actions. Retell the story (to yourself) as you go about your daily business. This may be supported with an audio recording that you make and listen to.

Telling the story of what happens when an oral mathematical story is taken to the classroom

I was daunted by the prospect of taking 'Little Lumpty' as an oral mathematical story to a class of 30 children aged five and six years. Eventually, the time comes to take what seems like a good, if little explored idea, over the edge, into reality. There is fear associated with going from the world of a research idea to the world of reality. If left as an idea for too long, it becomes too comfortable as a theory and then too uncomfortable to apply in the real world. There is a risk of finding that an idea just doesn't work: the original idea becomes broken. So over the edge I go, describing what happens when oral mathematical story telling as a theoretical idea is taken to the classroom.

Surprises

Little Lumpty comes out of a box and amazes the children. I am shocked to see 30 small children look at me with eyes wide. At one stage of the telling I am caught in a moment when we are bound together in the magic of the story. I worry that the children are becoming overly concerned about Little Lumpty. It is an amazing experience: thirty small children help create the number pattern as we count in twos.

About the class collectively the teacher, Lucy, notes:

'One hundred percent concentration throughout whole story.'

Children were one hundred percent focused for the whole of the story: 'fixated.'

(Walshe 2013)

Mathematical motivation

The motivation to provide the number sequence is evident as children join in with counting in multiples of two and as Casey (2011) notes motivation supports mathematical learning. By allowing time between counts I sense that this pattern is not secure and I need to provide words. I anticipated that this pattern would be secure and that support would be required beyond 20 for 22 and 24 but support is required for most of the count. However, the class teacher comments on how the children's motivation to provide the count number is high.

Making the mathematical idea explicit: a thinking string

I make the mathematical intention explicit before telling the story. I write the mathematical idea 'counting in multiples of two', which defines the mathematical idea of the story and read this out. I use the same principle of making the aim clear before starting a lecture when teaching Higher Education students. It is a way of framing the purpose and offers a reference to return to at the end. This approach to teaching transfers across to all ages. I think of it as a jam sandwich: bread-jam-bread. The aim is pitched, the idea developed and we seal it together by returning to the originally stated aim. This clarity of intention helps educator and learner.

Making the mathematical idea explicit crystallises the language of 'count in multiples of two' or 'count in twos' in our minds. I use a piece of string to physically join the written up mathematical idea with the book 'Little Lumpty' (Imai 1994): connecting story and mathematics. I ask children to imagine they have a thinking string and mention that I will later ask about it. This is challenging but it is interesting to note the response of a particular child to this idea.

At the start of the oral mathematical story I am aware that oral story relies on auditory senses and question whether it will suit children for whom this is challenging. The class teacher, Lucy, observes how individual children respond to this oral mathematical story experience. She notes how three children categorised as 'lower ability', autistic and a child acquiring English as a Second Language (ESL) surprise her. The names of these children have been changed.

Lower ability

It might be that children are categorised as lower ability because they are different. It could be that some children find that they are round pegs in square holes. There is a certain school culture that some children learn and even embrace but others don't. Patricia, a child considered as lower ability, responds to the oral mathematical story about counting in multiples of two in surprising ways. The first surprise is in how she responds to the 'thinking string' suggestion at the start of the story: she physically dramatises this idea, pulling an imaginary string away from the side of her head. She repeats this pulling action several times.

Thinking string

Patricia mimes to herself, a string going from her head

Class teacher notes this during storytelling

(McGrath 2013)

When the group is asked to think about the mathematics of the story, Patricia 'pretends to pull string again' and perceptively describes what is going on using mathematical language:

Story teller: 'What do you think about the mathematical ideas in the story?'
Patricia: 'When you counted in twos you missed one out, so it's like a pattern.'

(McGrath 2013)

It might be that oral story tells us something of children who do not fit into high ability groups. The class teacher expresses surprise at Patricia: she would never have thought this child would respond like this.

This child's thinking fits with a creative classroom experience combining mathematics and story. This mathematical experience disrupts the 'ability group' assumption made about Patricia. This child mimes pulling a thinking string from her head, explains counting in multiples of two as a 'pattern'. I realise this is a rare, never to be repeated moment. As one of 30 listening children, a lower ability child challenges her teacher's assumption of her mathematical ability.

Autistic child

On the occasion of telling 'Little Lumpty', a teaching assistant is available to encourage an autistic child's engagement. The assistant reads the picture book 'Little Lumpty' to James; he listens to the story and later represents Lumpty's ladder in a drawing. He tunes in to the difference between the picture book and my oral version. James takes the story idea of counting in multiples of two to his drawing. His supporting adult comments on how he engages with the story and, though he leaves part way, I am wrong in my assumption that the experience is not working for him; it is because he needs the toilet.

> James, who shows autistic characteristics, represents the ladder with many rungs and counts to 48 in twos with support. He tells me several times that Lumpty was left in 'one piece' whereas Humpty Dumpty is 'broken' and 'cannot be fixed'. James articulates counting beyond the twelfth multiple to the twenty-fourth multiple.
>
> (McGrath 2013)

English as a Second Language (ESL)

Monty, who is acquiring English as a second language, engages with the story experience in a surprising way. His class teacher describes how Monty is smiling and transfixed for the story. This is worth noting as I have a concern that oral mathematical story relies on auditory skills and receptive language.

> Monty – listening very intently – smiling at parts of story.
>
> (McGrath 2013)

Connecting the mathematical idea of counting in multiples to this story works well: harmony between the story and the mathematical idea engages children. I am struck with how the expression on children's faces is so animated and how eye contact is unwavering. Children connect to the story: introducing Little Lumpty is a key moment of excitement. Children respond positively to the prop characterisation of Lumpty and are motivated to help him count in twos, to steady his nerves and to find out how high the wall is.

Conclusion

There is risk associated with telling a version of 'Little Lumpty' to a class of 30 children aged between five and six years of age, exposing a research idea to the real world. Taking the risk reveals that it is possible to connect story and mathematical ideas in a creative way: a research egg rolls over the edge, unbroken.

This chapter fine-tunes relationships between story and unintentional mathematical ideas in the story 'Little Lumpty' (Imai 1994). A five-year-old child points out the counting opportunity, which is then developed to counting in multiples of two to the twelfth multiple.

Steps involved in moving from picture books to oral mathematical story versions are sketched out. Part of this process involves thinking in a connected way: seeing the possibilities for connections between story and mathematics and between mathematical ideas. Mathematical intentions are made explicit with a stretch of string a 'thinking string', physically connecting the book 'Little Lumpty' and the mathematical idea 'counting in multiples of twos' written on a small white board.

This creative pedagogical approach to teaching mathematics challenges teacher assumptions about some of these children. A child classed as 'lower ability' responds to the oral mathematical story in most surprising ways. She demonstrates pulling on an imaginary thinking string, which connects the story to the mathematical idea. She articulates the mathematical idea in an enlightening way. Her teacher tells me that she would not have expected such responses from this child. Combining oral story and mathematics disrupts the culture of this classroom in a positive way. Though I land safely on a creative mathematical blanket, I am left with the sense that more could happen here.

Oral mathematical story

Possibilities

Talking as a group is important for children: 'they learn best to become themselves through dialogue with others'.

(Fisher 2009, p.12, my italics)

This chapter aims to explore:

- the value of children talking in groups
- gauging children's genuine participation as part of oral mathematical story experiences
- adults supporting deeper mathematical connections.

🔊 'Two of Everything'

Retold by Suzanne Kelham

Mr Haktak and Mrs Haktak live in a little hut. They rely on whatever they can grow in their garden to survive. One morning Mr Haktak is digging his garden when his shovel strikes something hard, an ancient brass pot. As he carries the large pot indoors his purse, which contained his last five coins, falls in. Mrs Haktak didn't know what to make of the pot and, as she leans over to look in, her hair pin falls in. As she tries to retrieve it she finds two hairpins and two purses. Inside each purse are five coins. That night, Mr and Mrs Haktak fill and empty the pot until they have more money than they need. Next day, Mrs Haktak is embracing the pot in thanks when she gets a fright; Mr Haktak kicks the door open, his arms full with provisions, and she falls in. Mr Haktak pulls out two wives and this is when trouble starts to double. The solution is another Mr Haktak, and two of everything.

(adapted from Toy Hong 1993)

Introduction

This chapter considers the importance of children talking in groups to nourish individual mathematical development. Theoretical ideas are outlined in order to understand the importance of young children talking. Features of creative dialogue such as 'engagement' and 'participation', which were introduced in Chapter 4, are discussed in more detail.

Professional storytellers and educators describe their experiences of telling oral mathematical stories to large groups. Challenges of telling oral mathematical stories, facilitating creative mathematical dialogue, and gauging children's genuine participation are outlined. For the purpose of this discussion a group is considered large if there are 30 or more children.

Mathematical ideas of generalising and abstracting, introduced in Chapter 1, are highlighted here with a view to promote these as ways of encouraging children to make deeper mathematical connections beyond a story context, should such opportunities arise. Experience in this oral mathematical story project establishes the potential to generate connections between mathematical ideas; this is more easily achieved with smaller groups of children. However, this is not to diminish the value of children experiencing mathematical stories as part of larger groups. This chapter aims to highlight the scope of possibilities that oral mathematical storytelling brings as a creative approach to thinking about mathematics.

The value of children talking in groups: theoretical perspectives

Internalising mathematical ideas

Group discussions are important so that children share social experiences before internalising ideas. Children reconstruct ideas internally, a concept Vygotsky (1978, p.56) refers to as 'internalisation'. Vygotsky (1978) theorises that this happens when an interpersonal process is transformed into an intrapersonal one. Vygotsky (1978, p.57) describes how '[e]very function in the child's cultural development appears twice: first on the social level, and later, on the individual level; first, between people (inter psychological) and then inside the child (intra psychological)'. Oral mathematical story is first between people, before children reconstruct ideas individually.

Children in the project hear an oral mathematical story in a group, internalise these story ideas, and retell the mathematical story (see Chapter 9 for examples). Vygotsky (1978, p.57) describes how '[a]spects of external or communicative speech as well as egocentric speech turn 'inwards' to become the basis of inner speech'. I am struck by how accurately the language of the story is replicated when children take the role of storyteller. Mathematical language generated through oral story is external speech, which turns inwards to become the child's inner speech, and turns outwards when children retell stories. Children turn story speech that is mathematical outwards, as they retell story in their story play narratives (Chapter 3), and as storytellers (Chapter 9).

Talk unifies children's mathematical behaviour

Talk or speech unifies and organises many aspects of children's mathematical behaviour. In the afterword of Vygotsky (1978, p.126), Vera John-Steiner and Ellen Souberman comment that 'speech acts to organise, unify, and integrate many disparate aspects of children's behavior such as perception, memory, and problem solving'. Pound and Lee comment on 'how the brain is able to connect with story, and how narrative images expand in the brain, not only clarifying the gaps, but confining the information to memory' (2011, p.73). Story speech is important in that it allows children to perceive, remember and solve problems in a unified way.

Collective thinking nourishes individuals

Construction of shared knowledge and understanding contributes to individual understanding. Children strengthen their own understanding as a result of dialogue with others (Fisher 2009). Mercer (2000) makes the point that, unlike bees, children can use what they gather from collective experiences to further develop individual thinking:

> Human communication partners need not just take what the other gives and then go and carry out individual activities, as do the honey-bees; they can use information which has been shared as an intellectual resource, working on it to make better sense than they might alone.
>
> (Mercer 2000, p.172)

Children learn best to become themselves through interaction with others (Fisher 2009). Theoretical perspectives suggest that collective talking experiences nourish children's individual thinking (Fisher 2009; Mercer 2000; Vygotsky 1978).

Thoughts into words

By participating in dialogue children translate mathematical thoughts into words and expand their thinking: dialogue forces children to translate their thoughts into words. Dialogue can expand children's thinking by creating thoughts that they would not have had before (Fisher 2009), thus attributing value to the articulation of mathematical ideas in discussions and in play.

Key points:

- Children internalise ideas discussed in groups and these ideas contribute to individual understanding (Vygotsky 1978).

- Collective discussion nourishes children's individual thinking (Fisher 2009; Mercer 2000).
- Dialogue requires that children translate thoughts into words and therefore expands their thinking (Fisher 2009).
- Thinking as a group is important for children: 'they learn best to become themselves through dialogue with others' (Fisher 2009, p.12).

Creative mathematical dialogue

Conversations become creative when children think beyond what they already know: 'A dialogue becomes creative when it allows for playful and divergent ideas' (Fisher 2009, p.8). Dialogue is creative when it is about improvising and making connections between ideas and concepts that you have not thought of connecting before (Fisher 2009; Pound & Lee 2011). These connections may or may not be something adults have considered: children often make fresh connections that as adults we need to adjust our thinking to. This playful quality of creative dialogue can be part of oral story telling: story can be played with, diverging to new ideas.

Extracts of children's creative mathematical dialogue in large group discussions

> ### 'Stone Soup'
>
> Paula Brown tells an adapted version of 'Stone Soup' (Brown 2013b). She invites children to describe the vegetables before they are sliced and diced in the story. There are some imaginative mathematical descriptions: Broccoli is described as 'a tree shape'; celery as 'a rectangle' or 'a number one'; red cabbage 'a bit like a lovely pattern'; chickory as 'oval'; butternut squash as 'like an eight' or 'two circles joined together' describing this 3D shape using a 2D perspective.
>
> > (Forest 1998, offers a lovely version of this story)

It is interesting to note in the above example how children describe a 3D butternut squash using words for 2D shapes. Suggate *et al.* (2010; 2006) advise that it is not enough for children to think of shapes as wholes, and that children need to consider the properties of shapes. When the children were describing the 3D vegetables, it is as if they were seeing parts of the vegetables, i.e. one surface (face) of the squash, which, if sliced off, would resemble an eight. The story experience led to a creative description of 3D shapes using two dimensional terms and children need to see 3D shapes as essentially infinite layers of 2D shapes.

'Two of Everything'

Martha describes what Mr Haktak finds as 'a big magic pot, that if you put one in, it will turn into two, if your put four in, it will turn into six, I mean eight'.

Jacob explains why ten coins come out of the pot: 'Because five and five make ten'. Jacob says, 'Mr Haktak can become rich. He could have a thousand pounds'. Later Jacob suggests repeating the doubling action a thousand times. When two Mrs Haktaks are pulled out Jacob says, 'Now he's got two wives!'

(adapted from Toy Hong 1993)

Creative dialogue can be summed up as 'playful talk': playful with ideas, suggesting alternative possibilities and encouraging children to be imaginative in their thinking.

Creative dialogue as part of oral mathematical story supports children connecting ideas in a playful way. Oral story encourages creativity in mathematics; however, this creative approach to teaching mathematics brings challenges. One of the challenges is being able to gauge to what extent children are engaging or participating with the story experience particularly as part of large groups. Before describing views on gauging children's participation I identify three challenges facing the storyteller when working with larger groups.

Challenges of oral storytelling

There are three main reasons why the prospect of telling a story to communicate a mathematical idea feels challenging. First, we don't readily perceive ourselves as storytellers and may need to establish these skills, through practice. Second, managing 30 children is challenging, possibly even more so when coupled with storytelling without the support of a book. Third, it is potentially working in a spontaneous way that carries creative risk (Gallas 1995; Hartman 2002; Naik 2013). Added to this there are elements of unpredictability: children's responses will be unpredictable as we aim to encourage creative mathematics thinking; the environment (doors open and close sometimes for no apparent reason), unexpected events (for example a party of prospective parents being shown around). However, the challenges are worth it, as reflected in the words of an early years teacher: 'It has challenged that view of myself as not being very creative. It has opened up new possibilities' (Kelham 2013b).

Multiplicity of directions

Creative dialogue is more challenging to facilitate as we don't know which direction it might take. There could be mathematical ideas that unsettle us and need thinking about beyond the moment of the story. Fisher describes this feature of creative dialogue: 'It is generative and open-textured and has the potential to move in a multiplicity of directions and reach unexpected conclusions' (Fisher 2009, p.9). Suzanne, a Reception class teacher, describes how 'you don't know where it's going: that is its power and its most scary bit' (Kelham 2013b). This potential to go in many directions makes facilitating creative dialogue challenging, particularly with larger groups.

Nervousness

I notice how experienced teachers display nervousness before telling an oral mathematical story. Suzanne Kelham, an experienced early years teacher, explains this:

> Suzanne explains how oral mathematical storytelling is like a performance. It takes one out of one's comfort zone. It is a performance compared to the more usual narrative of teaching.
>
> (Kelham 2013b)

Other factors

There are other factors around telling oral mathematical stories to groups of children; Fisher (2009, p.128) identifies 'group size, behaviour of others, the roles they take on, their relationships, their motivation and effort'. Suzanne Kelham reflects on how she is more aware of managing behaviour when telling an oral mathematical story to a class of 30 than with smaller groups. She comments on her own behaviour in smaller groups, stating how she is more relaxed and freer. Telling a story to a larger group requires that the storyteller manages group dynamics and behaviour.

Gauging children's participation

Children as legitimate peripheral participants: genuine participation

Lave and Wenger (1991) describe how learning an apprenticeship such as midwifery involves legitimate peripheral participation. The learner is legitimately placed on the edge and starts learning about the profession from this position. Learners move in from the periphery as apprenticeships advance. Lave and Wenger (1991, p.32) describe how 'children are, after all, quintessentially legitimate peripheral participants in adult social worlds'. It strikes me that in larger groups children are peripheral participants and it is difficult to know whether they are participating or not participating, or behaving in a way that avoids attracting attention. Genuine participation that does not fit classroom behavioural expectations is described in the following extract:

'Two of Everything' by Toy Hong

'Two of Everything' is about a magic pot that doubles whatever falls in and is told to a group of 30 children aged five and six years old. Observing children collectively shows a girl playing with her hair in a distracted way, which goes without comment; a boy throws himself down as if he is falling into a magic pot to be doubled: the boy shows 'genuine' physical participation with the story but is participating in a physical way, which might not fit with classroom behaviour expectations. The girl may not be participating and her behaviour fits with expectations or she could be participating peripherally.

(McGrath 2013)

As legitimate peripheral participants (Lave & Wenger 1991) it is difficult for adults to know if children are participating in a genuine way. Whether individual children are genuinely participating or merely behaving in non-participatory ways, in keeping with classroom behavioural expectations, becomes more difficult to determine in large groups. Haynes and Murris (2012, p.209) describe how 'much recent research on pedagogy underlines the centrality of oracy and the importance of a culture of genuine participation, listening, and responding'. Non-participation can be disguised by children who learn 'to do school', behaving in low-level distracted ways.

Engagement

In Chapter 4 a summary of research shows that children's engagement improves when mathematical ideas are connected to story (Hong 1996; Keat & Wilburne 2009). This word 'engagement' deserves further discussion as it is often mentioned when I ask educators about how children respond to oral mathematical story. First I define what is meant by the word 'engagement' in the context of children listening or contributing to the dialogue of oral mathematical story. Fisher (2009, p.183) proposes that evidence for engagement is when a child 'shows consistent attention and interest in the dialogue'. This learning behaviour is seen when a child is '[c]onsistently responding to others' contributions and showing interest in the dialogue, though not necessarily saying much' (Fisher 2009, p.183).

A storyteller perspective

🔊 **'One City, Two Brothers'**

Retold by Paula Brown

Paula Brown tells a story based on 'One City, Two Brothers' (Smith 2007) to a group of 120 children aged between five and seven years of age. Later I invite Paula's thoughts on what she thinks about 'engagement' in the context of such a large group. Paula describes these large group tellings as more of a one hit wonder and identifies that you are not getting under the skin of it. Paula comments how at the time she never really knows what went in, or how this is affecting children; but she notes that some children remember these stories two or three years later. Smaller group work allows more stopping and exploring; more finding out about children's mathematical thinking.

(Brown 2013c)

Paula Brown makes the point that children as part of larger groups are engaging with the story but that as a storyteller it is difficult to gauge this (Brown 2013c). I found when telling 'Little Lumpty' to a group of 30 that I rely on the class teacher to record how collectively and individually children engage or participate.

The children in Figure 6.1 draw on clipboards while listening to an oral mathematical story. Figure 6.2 shows an example of a child's drawing, which represents her mathematical thinking. Figure 6.3 shows children engaging with a retelling of 'The Enormous Turnip'.

Adults can support deeper mathematical connections

I sense from observing professional storytellers and adults telling stories to groups of varying sizes that there are possibilities for connecting story and mathematics on different levels. The first level of connection is that of connecting story with a mathematical idea. The telling of 'Little Lumpty' to a group of 30 children achieves this (Chapter 5). The focus is on connecting one mathematical idea counting in multiples of two to the twelfth multiple, to a story about Lumpty who wants to succeed where Humpty Dumpty fails. By making the mathematical idea explicit at the start I pitch in children's minds what to be thinking of and am greeted with Patricia's perceptive comment about a pattern and how the count misses one out. A second level of connection that happened during the research project more naturally in smaller groups is thinking about what if something about the story or the mathematics changes. This level involves moving between mathematical ideas within the one story and playing with the story and/or the mathematics. A third level is projecting the mathematical idea beyond the

Figure 6.1 Children draw on clipboards while listening to an oral mathematical story (legitimate peripheral participants).

Figure 6.2 Nesta's clipboard drawing (five years and two months) represents ten spots and eight spots on a ladybird after listening to a version of 'Ladybird on a Leaf' where the mathematical ideas $5 + 5 - 5 = 5$ and $5 + 3 - 3 = 5$ are expressed.

story context. This is challenging as it involves realising there is a pattern or a mathematical idea that can be generalised, or that a mathematical idea can be extracted from the story context.

Children making imaginative generalisations

In the 'Ladybird on a Leaf' story, children explain using the story context that the rain washes away spots and the ant adds them on, but need support in extending explanations about mathematical ideas beyond this story context (Chapter 3). Drawing out explanations about what happens 'every' time is getting children to think like mathematicians (Haylock & Cockburn 2013). Children use story language to explain mathematical happenings, as Millie does in the example below; a point we will return to.

'Ladybird on a Leaf'

After hearing the 'Ladybird on a Leaf' story, Millie describes the mathematical pattern $N - n + n = N$ as: 'It was when the rain cloud washes off and the ant puts them back; and the rain cloud keeps washing them off and the ant keeps putting them back on.'

(McGrath 2013)

When the pattern of the story and pattern of the mathematical idea work well together, it is possible that children articulate the pattern in words and express this in play. However, opening out this third level of connection is not always easy and depends on the ability of the storyteller to think about and generalise mathematical ideas.

Storyteller can articulate generalisations

Young children may not find pattern recognition easy (Frobisher 1999) and might need support in articulating patterns in general terms beyond the story. Asking children to explain what is going on can lead to children making generalisations. Adults can articulate patterns for children. Seeing a pattern enables children to predict or to make generalisations as they realise that something will 'always' be the case.

Young children might not be able to explain mathematical thinking explicitly (Haylock & Cockburn 2013). As part of the oral storytelling experience it is valuable to make the mathematical thinking explicit at the start, during or after the story as discussed in Chapter 5, where emphasis is placed on being explicit at the start, and Chapter 8, when as part of telling 'The Elves and the Shoemaker' Rebecca steps away from the story to make the mathematical idea clear. This articulation of the mathematical idea gives a point of reference from which story-related mathematical ideas can be generalised and provides language to explain mathematical ideas.

Questions to prompt mathematical generalising

What is the pattern in the story?

Does that happen every time?

What do you think will happen next?

What pattern are you using (thinking about)?

How can you check that (props)?

(Adapted from Haylock & Cockburn 2013, p.299)

Abstraction

Abstraction makes a context irrelevant. To understand abstraction we could draw from an idea of irrelevance to counting: 'counting is an abstraction, so the actual objects counted are irrelevant to the process; the order of the objects is irrelevant; the arrangement of the objects is irrelevant' (Haylock & Cockburn 2013, p.61). The same counting process can be repeated in different contexts. To further support this point I take an example from Haylock and Cockburn (2013) and suggest that, as storytellers, we can think about how a mathematical idea, such as 12 is 9 more than 3, could be at the core of a story and abstracted by children:

Abstraction

Three stages in developing the use of the language of comparison can be identified. These are applied to an example of subtraction for comparison.

Stage 1

When comparing a line of cubes, a child notices 'more blue cubes than red cubes' and should be encouraged to note there are 'fewer red than blue'. No numbers are involved in these statements.

Stage 2

There are nine more blue cubes than red cubes or there are nine fewer red than blue, this time specifying the numerical difference.

Stage 3

The third stage is to make the abstracted statements: 12 is 9 more than 3 or 3 is 9 less than 12; the context is ignored and the child can make the abstracted statement.

(Haylock & Cockburn 2013, p.74)

Story provides a comfortable context for mathematical ideas. However, it is the extraction of the mathematical idea from this context that presents a challenge: 'A major challenge in learning to do mathematics is to learn to abstract the mathematical concept from the context in which they are embedded' (Haylock & Cockburn 2013, p.42). Offering play with story-related props is arguably still protecting the mathematical idea in a play story context. Inviting children to retell the story is also preserving the context. As Haylock and Cockburn (2013, p.43) point out, '[i]n a poem, a story, a picture, a song, a game, a piece of drama, and so on, the context is the essence of the activity', but for mathematics context is irrelevant, of little significance. I am proposing that the story or play offers a context to promote mathematical understanding but I acknowledge that the challenge is whether the ideas are understood so that they can exist or be realised beyond these contexts.

Positioning mathematical ideas in comfortable contexts presents two challenges: whether pattern or ideas can be generalised by children, and whether mathematical ideas can be separated out from story contexts by children. These are important challenges for us to think about when using oral mathematical story as a pedagogical tool to teach mathematics.

Figure 6.3 Children engaging as part of a retelling of 'The Enormous Turnip' with Kirsty Burns.

Children can be provided with a range of oral mathematical story experiences. Encouraging children to engage in creative dialogue, participate genuinely and generalise or explain a mathematical idea are possibilities of oral mathematical story experiences and are probably easier to achieve as outcomes of smaller group work.

Conclusion

This chapter considers children listening to oral mathematical story as one of a group of 30 or more. Vygotsky (1978) theorises that children need to think as part of a social group and proposes that in order for children to reconstruct ideas these need to be internalised by a child. This internalisation involves children in interpersonal and then intrapersonal thinking (Vygotsky 1978). Oral mathematical story and creative mathematical dialogue offer social experiences and ideas that can be internalised by children.

Participation for young children can be legitimately peripheral (Lave & Wenger 1991). The question to ponder is how can we know that children's participation is genuine (Haynes & Murris 2012) in larger groups, and whether this is easier to gauge with smaller groups.

Oral mathematical story invites playful dialogue. Fisher (2009) considers that dialogue becomes creative when it allows for playful and divergent ideas. Oral mathematical story that invites creative dialogue is challenging from the educator's perspective. One reason is because the mathematical dialogue can go in a multiplicity of directions reaching unexpected conclusions (Fisher 2009). This potential to go in many directions makes facilitating creative mathematical dialogue challenging. We want to disrupt children's mathematical thinking and, as Fisher (2009) suggests, we can do this through talk that extends, challenges and surprises.

Oral mathematical story experiences operate on many levels but, broadly speaking, within the first level there is a connection between an oral story and a mathematical idea; within the second level connections within mathematical ideas are made through particular examples and there can be connections between mathematical ideas working together within a story; within the third level the mathematical idea connects to pattern, which can be seen in a general way. Mathematics is about making connections (Haylock & Cockburn 2013; Haylock 2006; Suggate *et al.* 2010; 2006); oral storytellers can create experiences that allow children to make mathematical connections on different levels.

Oral mathematical story and creative dialogue brings challenges and surprises. Opening out oral story and creative mathematical dialogue in small groups is considered in the next chapter, where teachers Suzanne and Louise provide insight into telling story to groups of 30, and then smaller groups of four to eight children.

Oral mathematical story

Large and small groups

A Faery Song

'Give to these children, new from the world,
Rest far from men.
Is anything better, anything better?
Tell us it then'

(Yeats 1912)

This chapter aims to explore:

- opening out oral mathematical story to smaller groups
- prompting possibility thinking through creative dialogue
- children's response to small group oral storytelling.

◀)) 'The Greedy Triangle'

Retold by Suzanne Kelham

A triangle becomes dissatisfied with life. The triangle goes to a shape witch and asks for 'one more side and one more corner'. The triangle is happy being a square until dissatisfaction sets in and it asks the shape witch for 'one more side and one more corner', turning into a pentagon. This is fine until the pentagon feels dissatisfied and asks for 'one more side and one more corner', turning into a hexagon. It is then that the hexagon shape realises that actually it was happy as it was and returns to the shape witch to become a pentagon, then a square and finally a triangle.

(adapted from Burns 1994)

Introduction

After I retell 'Little Lumpty' to a group of 30 children several times, I sense that though the pattern of counting is stronger, an opportunity is missed: to connect more closely to children's mathematical behaviour. This chapter aims to explore what happens when oral mathematical stories are told to smaller groups of six to eight children. This chapter is based on a story adapted from a picture book *The Greedy Triangle* (Burns 1994) and a story about a dinosaur created by a Reception class teacher. Mathematical dialogue as part of these storytellings is imaginative and extracts are included to support the idea that creative dialogue is sometimes more easily facilitated as part of smaller group experiences.

This chapter draws upon perspectives of educators as storytellers and what they note about children's responses. Two Reception class teachers share their thoughts about telling the same story, 'The Greedy Triangle' (Burns 1994), to groups of 30 children and to smaller groups of six or eight children. For whole class story experiences, Suzanne skillfully tells the story of the triangle changing to a square, to a pentagon, to a hexagon, then reversing this sequence, hexagon, pentagon, square, triangle with 30 children. She combines this oral telling with the use of small straws and a visualiser connected to an interactive white board. Children see the triangle changing shape as the witch adds 'one more side and one more corner'. Louise dresses shapes up, attaching these to sticks like puppets. Louise shares her witch's hat and fully embraces the role of shape witch (see Figure 7.1).

Reflective thoughts of two Reception class teachers on telling 'The Greedy Triangle' to large and small groups of children:

Louise Cheshire holds the view that whether the story is better told to a larger group of 30, or to a smaller group of six or eight, depends on the story. She supports this point with examples. Her adapted version of 'My Cat Likes to Hide in Boxes' lends itself more readily to smaller groups, as children can handle the boxes. 'The Greedy Triangle' story works well with a whole class or a smaller group. She is comfortable telling this story to groups of 30 or less. Louise's telling of the shape story is supported with strong repetitive phrases, actions and dressed up shapes. Louise likes the buzz of telling stories to groups of 30 children but makes the point that this depends on the nature of the story and associated props.

(Cheshire 2013)

Figure 7.1 Louise Cheshire (Reception class teacher) retelling 'The Greedy Triangle'.

From this perspective it is noted that the larger group telling has its place and works better for some stories than others. The experience of listening to a story as one of a group differs for children as the group size varies. There is the potential to offer a range of oral mathematical experiences, with stories selected and adapted accordingly.

Opening out oral mathematical story to smaller groups

Small group work complements whole class teaching. Fisher (2009) proposes that '[t]raditional teacher–pupil interaction is a necessary feature of learning, but it is not sufficient, nor is it the best means for maximising the learning potential of children' (Fisher 2009, p.12). Suzanne Kelham, Reception class teacher, considers that there is 'something about the intensity of a small group', which suggests that small group work complements the more traditional interaction of whole class teaching.

Figure 7.2 Suzanne (Reception class teacher) relaxed and confident as a storyteller.

A freer and more relaxed storyteller

It is more challenging to manage the dynamics of a group of 30 young children; guiding genuine participation competes with managing the behaviour of larger groups. This whole class pedagogical approach positions the teacher higher (usually on a chair) than the children (sitting on the carpet).

Reflections on experience telling an adapted version of 'The Greedy Triangle' (Burns 1994)

Suzanne reflects on video recordings of her telling 'The Greedy Triangle' to a class of 30 children and to a smaller group of eight children. Suzanne describes how when telling 'The Greedy Triangle' to a group of 30 children she is more aware of the need to establish 'behaviour for learning'. Suzanne comments about her behaviour with smaller groups 'in my behaviour I am more relaxed and freer'. She is liberated from managing the behaviour of a larger group, which in turn allows her freedom. [See Figure 7.2.]

(Kelham 2013b)

'Alongside'

The benefit of working with smaller groups of children is that the educator can be 'alongside' children. Haynes and Murris advise that student teachers should experience working alongside children:

> Above all, student teachers need to know what it means to be alongside children, listening to them, happy in their company, able to enjoy mutually enriching conversation and exchanges of experience and perspectives, not immediately seeking to form and shape their futures through direct teaching.
>
> (Haynes & Murris 2012, p.229)

This idea of being 'alongside' transposes to telling oral mathematical stories to smaller groups of six or eight children.

When Suzanne tells stories to smaller groups of four and five year olds, she sits on the carpet with the children (see Figure 7.3). Sitting on the same level as children is physically 'being alongside one another' with the possibility that educator and child might influence each other (Haynes & Murris 2012; Coles 2013a; Coles 2013b). Oral

Figure 7.3 Suzanne (Reception class teacher) sitting 'alongside' children as a story listener.

mathematical storytelling with small groups, ideally away from the main classroom, creates a different learning experience. It is easier to hear, easier to encourage individual contributions, easier to spot opportunities for making mathematical connections or generalisations. Physically sitting alongside a smaller group fits with the intention to build an oral mathematical story with children.

Suzanne notices how the ritual of these small group storytelling sessions becomes established. Children choose to be part of these groups, sit on the cushions and remove their shoes. When children take the role of storyteller there is value in the adult sitting on a cushion as part of the audience as a story-listener, acknowledging the value the adult attaches to the child's role as storyteller.

Fresh connections

Extract of creative mathematical dialogue following the storytelling of 'The Greedy Triangle' (Burns 1994) retold by Louise Cheshire

Louise asks what if the shape was a square and kept growing outwards: imagine if he kept growing and growing and growing . . .

'Ice cube!' says Mikey.
'If he growed like this (shows fingers) he would be a diamond', Mikey demonstrates with fingers.
'I could change the hexagon into a pentagon', says another child.
'I could change the square into a diamond', says Mikey.
'Or what about a circle?' suggests another child.
'Or what about 4D?' another child proposes.

By its nature, oral mathematical story embraces dialogic teaching. Fisher distinguishes this way of teaching when he states that '[d]ialogic teaching is not just getting children to say what they think but is also challenging them to be creative and to think in new ways' (Fisher 2009, p.9). Creative dialogue following 'The Greedy Triangle' story challenges children to imagine a triangle turning into a circle, a square growing out and out into a cube or cuboid. In the discussion following 'The Greedy Triangle' children make connections between 2D and 3D shapes imagining a square growing into a cube. These are exciting creative mathematical ideas leading to one child asking about the possibility of a 4D shape. These connections were not necessarily what Louise the class teacher had in mind before telling the story: children make fresh connections, to which adults need to adjust their thinking.

Modelling dialogic habits

As part of storytelling educators can model good habits of dialogue. Fisher makes the point that '[w]hen teaching *through* dialogue teachers are also teaching *about* dialogue by modelling the habits of dialogue that children may learn to copy. Teachers create dialogic models' (Fisher 2009, p.107; italics in original). Modelling is achieved through repeated demonstration; active listening; questioning to prompt and probe; showing how to share ideas and seek alternative viewpoints (Fisher 2009). I note in the 'Blue Egg Dinosaur' story (which we come to shortly) how Suzanne carefully prompts possibility thinking with the children. Children learn about mathematical possibilities for the number eight, but also something about dialogue.

Small group work for oral mathematical story can be summarised as follows:

- A storyteller is freer and more relaxed as potentially there are less competing demands.
- Small group experience naturally positions an educator 'alongside' children.
- Small group oral mathematical story complements whole class teaching.
- Associated creative dialogue allows children to make fresh connections.

Prompting possibility thinking through creative dialogue

The quality of the oral mathematical story experience for the child will depend on the qualities of the story and skills of the adult as storyteller. Parkinson states:

> There may be some qualities intrinsic to a story and its structure, with other qualities emerging through the way the story is told that are still vital to the deeper engagement it creates – which is where storytelling rather than story reading or script performance retains advantages of flexibility and adjustment.
>
> (Parkinson 2011, p.12)

The flexible and adjustable nature of oral story set this experience apart from reading story text.

Flexible thinking

Flexibility of oral story is expressed when storytellers play with the plot, inviting children's ideas. Flexible thinking (Naik 2013; Parkinson 2011; Stanford 2012) is achieved by keeping some of the story content open (for example not specifying but inviting number pattern or relationships ideas) and by inviting changes to the story plot to disrupt the relationship between story and mathematics. What if the greedy triangle wants to become a circle? What will the shape witch need to do?

We now follow an account of Suzanne telling a story based on addition to a small group of children. She supports the storytelling with props, which are set out before children arrive: two baskets, each with four blue dinosaur eggs. During this story Suzanne skillfully asks questions in ways that prompt possibility thinking.

◀)) 'Blue Egg Dinosaur' story

Told by Suzanne Kelham

Once upon a time there was a tiny dinosaur called Jack-O-Saurus. The thing that Jack-O-Saurus loved to do was to jump; he jumped and he jumped and he jumped. He especially liked to try and catch dragonflies. When he saw a dragonfly he would jump and jump and jump. The dragonfly would fly higher and higher. One day he was down by the river when he saw a dragonfly fluttering, so he jumped and he jumped and he jumped. But the dragonfly flew quickly into the forest and he decided to chase it. And he ran, and he ran, and he ran. All of a sudden he tripped over. He didn't see two dinosaur nests. He knocked all of the eggs out of the nests. 'Oh no! If the scary dinosaur comes back and I tripped over his nests he might eat me!' So he puts the eggs back in the baskets but thinks; 'I don't know how many are meant to be in each nest.'

(Kelham 2013c)

Mathematical ideas in the 'Blue Egg Dinosaur' story

Before reading transcripts from the small group oral mathematical story experience we look at mathematical ideas that connect to the story. Understanding something about these mathematical ideas strengthens our position as oral mathematical storytellers. Haylock and Cockburn (2013) offer clear explanations, as do other authors of mathematical texts, getting under the skin and telling the story of mathematical ideas clearly.

Addition structures

Addition as the union of two sets refers to 'situations in which objects in two sets are collected together in some way' (Haylock & Cockburn 2013, p.64). The dinosaur story has two baskets of blue eggs: 'two distinct sets of objects, are brought together to form what is called the *union of the two sets,* and the cardinal number of this new set is computed' (Haylock & Cockburn 2013, p.64; italics in original). Two discrete sets are combined into one set: this story keeps the sets separate and invites the child to think about combining numbers of eggs. Haylock and Cockburn (2013, p.65) advise that 'the union of two distinct sets into one is an important structure that has to be linked with the symbols and language of addition; it forms part of the network of connections that constitutes the concept of addition'.

Haylock and Cockburn (2013, p.65) describe another addition structure as 'counting on and increasing'. This invites children to keep one amount in their heads and to count on the other amount. Bringing these two structures together, 'union of two sets' and 'counting on', is an important stage in developing understanding about addition (Haylock & Cockburn 2013, p.67). The mathematical ideas of 'union of two sets' and 'counting on' lie at the heart of the 'Blue Egg Dinosaur' story, along with another idea: commutative principle of addition.

Commutative principle of addition

For any two numbers, a and b:

if $a + b = c$ then $b + a = c$

or

$a + b = b + a$

The order in which two numbers are written makes no difference to the result. This principle is important in understanding structure of addition and makes calculations more accessible (Haylock & Cockburn 2013, p.123). Realising this pattern or generalisation leads to the strategy that when adding two numbers together we can start with the larger and add or count on the smaller number ($100+5=5+100$). We are better keeping the number 100 in our heads and counting on five. These realisations are important as they more readily facilitate mathematical manipulations. The 'Blue Egg Dinosaur' story extends these addition ideas along with another mathematical idea: complements of a number.

Complements of a number

Patterns of number complements support children's mental mathematical manipulations. Complements of ten can be expressed as 'making a number up to ten': three and seven are ten-complements, because they add up to ten. Haylock and Cockburn (2013, p.144) advise that ideally we need to know the complements not just for making numbers up to ten, but for every number at least from 0 to 20. For the dinosaur story, complements of eight are:

$0 + 8 = 8$ $5 + 3 = 8$
$1 + 7 = 8$ $6 + 2 = 8$
$2 + 6 = 8$ $7 + 1 = 8$
$3 + 5 = 8$ $8 + 0 = 8.$
$4 + 4 = 8$

Children should be encouraged to be systematic and to look for and use pattern (Haylock & Cockburn 2013). Suzanne encourages children to record the possibilities on blank paper attached to clip boards. This is purposeful recording, helping children to put down what has been discovered so that they find more possibilities. This idea of systematic recording, Suzanne notes later, needs developing beyond this one storytelling.

Possibility thinking

Suzanne poses the question to think of ways of making eight: what are the possible complements of eight that can be represented by the eggs in the two baskets? Children find their way to some of these possibilities, which they are encouraged to record so that new possibilities are considered: it is easier to seek new possibilities if you record as you gather. Questioning is open and directed to the group rather than individuals. Suzanne reflects on how children are more encouraged to respond as there is no right or wrong answer: instead of asking what three and five make, it is about finding out possible ways of making eight, one of which is three and five. This story draws out some possibilities: more possibilities can be gathered in future tellings of this story. Children are left with the sense that not all possibilities have been discovered, that there are more.

Extracts of conversation between storyteller and children

So we've got eight altogether: three in this nest and five in that nest.
But Jack-O-Saurus is a little worried because it might be a different way.
Lexie says, 'put one, two, three, four, in one nest and one, two, three, four in the other nest'.
Ruan confirms, 'that makes eight'.
So we've got two different ways. I am going to find it hard to remember all the different ways.
Children get clip boards to note down the different ways.
So Jack-O-Saurus looks at the four eggs in one basket and the four in the other and he thought, 'but what if this isn't right? What if the dinosaur had more eggs in one nest than the other one?'
A child arranges a three and a five but in the opposite way to that of earlier and says, 'but last time there was five in this one and three in that one'.
Austen draws a question mark and says, 'a question for the story?'
Jack-O-Saurus knows it can be three and five or four and four but is really worried.

Ruan suggests a two and six arrangement but miscounts. Felix checks but also makes an error saying seven. Children recheck the number by arranging the eggs in a straight line.

Austen poses the question, 'what if it's the wrong way round and you have to swop it?'

So we've got six and two so eight altogether, or two and six (Suzanne following up on Austen's suggestion to swop).

A child suggests, 'we could have four and four and run away'.

Ruan: 'I think we need to check if they are the right dinosaur's.'

How?

'Smash them open', Ruan suggests.

Another child says, 'I know, stay there until the dinosaur comes, and say sorry'.

(Kelham 2013c)

'Blue Egg Dinosaur' story

Flexible telling of story alongside children explores some number complement possibilities, makes connections between addition structures (Haylock & Cockburn 2013) and allows children to make mathematical connections in a meaningful context. Through creative mathematical dialogue, the 'Blue Egg Dinosaur' story connects the following mathematical ideas: addition structures (combining two sets and counting on); commutative property of addition; complements of number eight.

Children responding to small group oral mathematical story

Quieter children

In smaller oral mathematical story situations, some children express and contribute more to mathematical discussion: 'The smaller the group the more chance children have, as individuals, to have their voice heard and to contribute to group effort' (Fisher 2009, p.128). I show a video clip of a child retelling an oral mathematical story and his teacher reflects how in whole class situations this child is quiet. His class teacher notes how 'oral mathematical storytelling suits his way of learning. It offers him his love of narrative'. Smaller group oral mathematical experiences allow children's voices to be heard.

Children who are quiet in more traditional learning contexts are noted as showing confidence when engaging with oral mathematical story in smaller groups. Louise reflects on how one child appears more confident when taking on the persona of a story character. Suzanne comments how Jessica partakes in the 'Blue Egg Dinosaur' story; normally she is quiet in the whole class learning situation. Without speaking, Jessica rearranges the eggs in the baskets contributing to the story in a physical way. Small group contexts allow quieter children the chance to be mathematically engaged in ways that larger group situations may not facilitate.

Accessing mathematical ideas

Children who are considered of lower ability, or who are at an earlier stage of mathematical development, can access mathematical ideas through oral story worlds. From discussions with Suzanne and Louise I note how oral mathematical story offers a way in for some children. One boy listens to 'The Elves and the Shoemaker', which is told with the mathematical intention to think about odd and even numbers (see Chapter 8). He joins in with the phrase 'not one, not two but three elves'. He accesses mathematical ideas about odd and even numbers on some level. This child may go away, as Suzanne suspects, with the idea of an even number needing a friend: a mathematical principle for even numbers.

Story language to explain mathematical ideas

Oral mathematical story is a language-based activity. Mathematical language is so much a part of oral mathematical storytelling. Suzanne describes how mathematical language flows along with story narrative rather than being stilted, as it can be with other teaching approaches; in fact, as Suzanne says, 'mathematical language becomes high profile'. Louise notices how one child uses the language of the story 'Two of Everything' (Toy Hong 1993) to explain his mathematical idea: 'I imagined I put them in the pot and they doubled.' Mathematical and story language works together to support children's explanations. I note in Chapter 6 how children use story language to describe mathematical ideas and explain the number pattern $N - n + n = N$. Further examples of children using story language to explain mathematical ideas include the following:

'Ladybird on a Leaf'

Ruan proposes, 'if she had five spots on, the rain could wash three away and the ant would put them back on. If she had five spots and the ant put two on the rain cloud would wash them off and she would have the same amount'. Ruan adds, 'the ladybird didn't realise the spots were coming off. The ant kept putting them on'.

Weather imagery encourages children to describe subtracting and adding of ladybird spots. Jessica describes how 'lots of heavy thunder came' and uses this image to remove ten spots. Toby describes 'soft rain' and removes one spot from ten leaving nine. Netta describes the pattern of the story as 'sunny, rainy, sunny, rainy'. Sony says that 'the cloud took the spots off and the ant put them on'. Max decides that his ladybird needs 'more spots' and states 'I need that sun!'

Mae poses a question in relation to the ladybird's problem with her artificial spots and the unpredictability of the weather: 'What if it rained in the middle of the day, but was sunny to start?'

'Little Lumpty'

Marnie describes Lumpty's perspective: 'He sat on the wall to see all the bits of the world. He saw the train station, his car. He saw someone flying their kite. He went back down the ladder.'

'Handa's Return Journey'

'Handa's Return Journey' is based on the original story 'Handa's Surprise' (Browne 1998): children listen to a story about Handa returning to her own village with her friend Akeyo.

In a retelling, Mya describes fruit falling from trees as Handa and Akeyo pass by with the basket. Mya imaginatively describes how Handa and Akeyo 'came past a banana tree and one fell in. Then an avocado tree . . .' When tangerines fall from a tree she describes, 'first, then another' (adding 14 tangerines).' Mya has a mixture of seven exotic fruit and 14 tangerines together in her basket and as part of her story sets about separating these out: 'I did have (separates out exotic fruit) . . . I didn't have (refers to little oranges).' Mya describes how 'Ostrich takes them as if they were her eggs'.

Children acquiring English as a second language

Repetitive phrases and actions are like hooks, connecting children into storytellings. Repetitive phrases are identified by Suzanne and Louise as important components of oral storytellings, which is a view held by Hartman (2002), Lipman (1999), Allison (1987) and Bryant (1947). As well as repetitive phrases the story can be retold and this repetition serves to bring familiarity with story and mathematical ideas. Children acquiring English as a second language are particularly supported by repetitive phrases and actions as part of storytellings.

A more detailed discussion with Suzanne and Louise reveals how a child's response depends on how much understanding of English the child has. For one particular child, pre-tutoring about the mathematical ideas is necessary before the story is told. This child has tutoring about what a triangle is, associated language and concepts of the story in his mother tongue first. This enables him to have some knowledge about what he is saying when joining in with the story.

The outcome of these discussions is that it is easier to really share thinking in small groups and 'dialogue becomes creative when thinking is shared' (Fisher 2009, p.10). I note how deeper mathematical engagement is brought about by the more intimate quality of small group story experiences. However, smaller group situations offer creative possibilities only when storytellers invite them.

Conclusion

In this chapter the educator as storyteller is alongside children both physically and attitudinally (Haynes & Murris 2012): the storyteller sits with children and is receptive to story and mathematical ideas from children. These experiences evoke creative mathematical dialogue as children make fresh connections: a triangle turning into a circle; a square turning into an 'ice cube'.

The shape of the story is likely to be more fluid than it would be for a whole class telling with 30 children. Suzanne, a Reception class teacher, uses the flexible quality of oral storytelling, posing questions that prompt mathematical thinking: what other ways are there to arrange eight eggs in two nests? Children record some possibilities but sense that there are more. Suzanne constructs this story with children in a way that prompts possibility thinking.

Children who are quieter in whole-class situations are willing to contribute to these discussions. This creative approach allows less able children to access mathematical ideas. Children acquiring English as a second language respond positively to stories with repetitive phrases and actions. Props are vital to support mathematical ideas as part of these experiences, a point considered in Chapter 8.

Small group observations show evidence of children's individual mathematical thinking. Children who are not usually noted for their contributions in larger group situations open up in these storytellings. Smaller group situations offer possibilities for playful mathematical and story dialogue. A more intimate, less predictable mathematical dialogue between storyteller and story listeners makes oral mathematical storytelling powerful and challenging as a complementary pedagogical choice.

Puppets and props

Mathematical stories in their making

Among School Children

O chestnut-tree, great-rooted blossomer,
Are you the leaf, the blossom or the bole?
O body swayed to music, O brightening glance,
How can we know the dancer from the dance?

(Yeats 1928)

The aims of this chapter are to explore how puppets and props:

- connect story, mathematics, storyteller and listener in purposeful ways
- are mathematical stories themselves
- nourish relationships between children, mathematical stories and storytellers.

◁)) 'The Elves and the Shoemaker'

Retold by Rebecca Belsten

Once upon a time there was a poor shoemaker. There was much competition in the town and he struggled to sell his shoes. He had only one piece of leather left and had no money for more. He set about making his last pair of shoes but left these unfinished overnight. The next morning he found the shoes finished. These sold quickly for a good price. He bought food and more leather. He started on new shoes and once again these were finished overnight and sold for good prices. He and his wife decided to stay up one night and watch to see who helps them. They find that elves have been helping them. They set about making clothes and shoes for the elves, who were delighted to find these wrapped as gifts. The shoemaker's success continued without the help of the elves.

(adapted from Grimm Brothers 1995)

Figure 8.1 Props made by Rebecca Belsten for 'The Elves and the Shoemaker'.

Introduction

A puppet is 'a model of a person or animal which can be moved either by strings or by a hand inside it' whereas a prop is 'a source of support or assistance' (Oxford Dictionary 2012). In the context of oral storytelling we consider a puppet as a representation of a story character and a prop as something that supports a story or mathematical idea in some way. These terms are used loosely and interchangeably in this context.

Puppets and props, like pictures of characters in illustrated books (Keat & Wilburne 2009), motivate children. Oral stories require children to abstract meaning from words, and puppets or props support this experience. Some puppets and props make story and mathematical ideas explicit, as they help children visualise what would otherwise need to be imagined.

Two Early Childhood Studies foundation degree students set about designing, creating and telling mathematical stories with their puppets and props. Their accounts give insights into how these puppets and props support mathematical ideas. Retelling 'The Elves and the Shoemaker', Rebecca Belsten connects story to understanding odd and even numbers, using the principle of pairing (Belsten 2013a). Retelling 'Goodnight

Gorilla', Rachel Adcock connects to ordinal value of numbers and sequencing of six animals in order. Puppets and props support these stories: the shoemaker, his wife and the elves capture the imagination of children with their fine detail, and shoes show numbers as odd or even (see Figure 8.1); a gorilla hand puppet draws children in, and a bunch of keys show ordinality of first, second, third, fourth, fifth and sixth. Imaginative qualities of these puppets and props spark creative mathematical dialogue during and after these stories, as children enquire as to how they were made.

This chapter aims to tell accounts of how educators support oral mathematical stories with puppets or props. The puppets or props have a connective purpose: children connect to the story and are mathematically motivated; the abstract nature of oral story is made concrete where props make mathematical ideas visual; storytellers have a 'comfort blanket' (Belsten 2013b), which helps their confidence. Puppets and props can be put to one side for later retellings.

Making puppets or props creates another mathematical story that can be shared with or enjoyed by children. A guide to making the shoemaker, his wife and the elves and five pairs of shoes helps Rebecca tell this story to children aged four and five, who are fascinated that she made these. The chapter starts with the connective purpose of props, looks at specific examples connecting stories and mathematical ideas, moves to creative stories about making props and puppets and concludes by commenting on the roles of props and puppets in nourishing relationships between children, mathematical stories and storytellers.

Connecting story, mathematics, storyteller and listener in a purposeful way

The representation of story characters with puppets motivates children to engage with mathematical activity. A prop or puppet is some concrete representation of story and mathematical abstraction. They can provide concrete expressions of abstract mathematical ideas. Puppets and props connect story, mathematics, teller and listener.

Puppet characters: mathematical motivation

Children's mathematical motivation is enhanced by story characters. Keat and Wilburne (2009) find that story characters motivate children in their mathematical achievement. Representing an oral story character with a puppet activates enthusiastic engagement in learning in a similar way to illustrated characters in books (Keat & Wilburne 2009). Puppets motivate children to construct mathematical meaning: children want to help story characters. Children are motivated to help Little Lumpty count in multiples of two to the twelfth multiple (2, 4, 6, 8, 10, 12, 14, 16, 18, 20, 22, 24) though the pattern of number names is not automatic and is challenging for the majority.

Abstract to concrete: making mathematical ideas explicit

Egan (1988) proposes that not all learning needs to move from concrete to abstract, as is generally considered the case for young children (Chapter 2). There is potential for young children to learn in a different way: moving from abstract to concrete. Children can listen to the mathematical ideas of a story and play with story-related props, expressing ideas in a concrete way. Abstract mathematical and story ideas connect through oral story and story-related props can support construction of mathematical ideas.

Visualisation of mathematical ideas

Young children manage the abstract nature of an oral story, and this experience can be supported with puppets or props. For very young children, puppets and props capture the imagination and offer a connection to the essence of the mathematical story. Story-related props help children construct mathematical ideas. Hughes (1986 p.47, italics in original) presents Patrick, aged 4 years and 1 month, with a series of questions. When asked questions like 'how many is two *lollipops* and one more?', Patrick responds correctly but when asked the abstract question, 'how many is two and one more?', Patrick responds incorrectly. Construction of story and mathematical

Example of props making mathematical ideas visual

In a telling of 'Handa's Return Journey' (based on original story 'Handa's Surprise' (Browne 1998), Handa returns home with five tangerines in an open basket and the storyteller arranges and rearranges these in ways that allow mathematical subtraction complements to be expressed in concrete ways. In a story retelling, a monkey takes five tangerines but then changes his mind and replaces these, deciding to run away instead. Another animal takes four tangerines leaving one in the basket but then changes its mind after deciding this is too greedy, replaces the four and takes only one of the five tangerines and so on.

Five tangerines can show subtraction complements as follows:

$5 - 5 = 0; 5 - 0 = 5.$

$5 - 4 = 1; 5 - 1 = 4;$

$5 - 2 = 3; 5 - 2 = 3;$

In 'Ladybird on a Leaf', removing and replacing velcro spots on the back of the ladybird makes the pattern $N - n + n = N$ or $N + n - n = N$ visual.

meaning can be assisted by props, as children visualise mathematical ideas at the core of the story through the supporting materials.

When Rebecca tells the story of 'The Elves and the Shoemaker' she uses props that she made to support the story context and the mathematical idea of odd and even, based on the principle of pairing, which is natural with a pair of shoes (see Figure 8.2).

There are two ways to approach the odd and even characteristic of number: partitioning into two equal groups or grouping into twos (McGrath 2010, p.78). Frobisher (1999) advises that children need to experience both partitioning into equal sets and dividing into sets of twos so that children can see odd and even patterns in numbers. The principle of pairing (Merttens 1987) is something that children can do in practical ways. Rebecca uses the idea of pairing to explore odd and even numbers. Initially this pairing is more obvious by using matching shoes but she also uses non-matching shoes to show that the idea is about the number and not the shoe.

Figure 8.2 Children enjoying the story props and 'not one, not two but three elves' seeing even and odd numbers.

Account of 'The Elves and the Shoemaker' retold by Rebecca Belsten

Rebecca tells the story of the shoemaker who is helped by the elves. Each time she takes the little elves out she says, 'not one, not two, but three elves', and children join in with this repetitive phrase. A repeated sequence leads to five pairs of shoes being placed on an imaginary shelf. Rebecca is careful to line the pairs up so children see clearly the total number of shoes. The five pairs of shoes amaze children.

Creative mathematical dialogue

It is interesting to note how in one retelling Rebecca makes the mathematical idea of the story explicit part way through the telling, and yet this does not detract from the story experience. It is as if she steps to the side of the story, using story context to hold a mathematical dialogue. Two minutes later, she returns to the telling. Rebecca starts this mathematical discussion with a question, which generates a wonderful reply:

'Have you heard of odd or even numbers?' Rebecca asks.

'I've heard of them when I was three', a child replies.

Mathematical ideas expressed in this retelling of 'The Elves and the Shoemaker'

Counting in ones and twos: some children count in ones, but the pairs of shoes prompt others to count in twos.

Total number and number of pairs: children realise the interchange between total numbers of shoes and number of pairs: ten shoes are five pairs; eight shoes equate with four pairs; six shoes equate with three pairs; four shoes equate with two pairs; two shoes equate with one pair.

Even and odd: children see number relationships with these shoes: the idea of a number being seen as made up of pairs if even and incomplete pairs if odd. Putting three shoes together children can see the oddness of three. One child says 'four is made up of two evens': perceiving the number four as being made up of pairs. Rebecca then uses shoes that do not match (odd shoes) to show how the nature of the shoe does not matter to the oddness or evenness of the number. Children click onto the idea of the principle of pairing and I hear a child utter 'definitely even'.

(McGrath 2013)

Another student, Rachel, retells 'Goodnight Gorilla' using a hand puppet to represent the gorilla, a bunch of six keys and a photograph of an armadillo. The gorilla hand puppet is used to introduce the story character (see Figure 8.3).

Figure 8.3 Rachel Adcock introducing 'Goodnight Gorilla' using the gorilla hand puppet she made.

◀)) 'Goodnight Gorilla'

Retold by Rachel Adcock

This story is about a gorilla who snatches the zoo keeper's set of six keys and lets five other animals out of their cages. A gorilla, an elephant, a hyena, a lion, a giraffe and an armadillo find themselves in the zoo keeper's bedroom before being returned to the zoo by his wife, who a child describes as 'annoyed'. Children recall this sequence of six animals in order along with ordinal language: first, second, third, fourth, fifth, sixth.

Rachel starts by explaining to children the mathematical idea of her story. She describes how it will be about remembering the order of animals. The mathematical idea is made explicit before the story starts. Children are aware of the purpose of the story and what to think about.

Rachel starts the story with a hand puppet, which represents the gorilla. She invites children to think of other zoo animals and associated actions. This storytelling requires children to follow the gorilla in a circle. Children enjoy the physical aspect of this story. Children recall the sequence of six animals as they are locked up in their cages.

The story builds up:

Gorilla
Gorilla + Elephant
Gorilla + Elephant + Hyena
Gorilla + Elephant + Hyena + Lion
Gorilla + Elephant + Hyena + Lion + Giraffe
Gorilla + Elephant + Hyena + Lion + Giraffe + Armadillo

(adapted from Rathmann 2012)

'Key' counting strategies

There is a correlation between number of keys and number of animals. I notice how in one telling when a child is given the bunch of keys to count he applies a practical strategy of bunching up the keys he counts, separating these out from those not yet counted. In another telling a boy leaves the keys flat on the ground and miscounts seven instead of six. Rachel addresses this by requesting that the count is checked.

Memory

In one storytelling Rachel incorrectly rebuilds the sequence of animals above, which goes unnoticed by the children or herself: as adults we make errors.

Children need support recalling the sequence of six animals in the correct order. Ordering in this way requires children to remember, to store this sequential addition in their minds. The associated actions, for example waving an arm in front for an elephant's trunk, work well to support recall. George, one of the youngest children, shows this arm waving action when children are asked what the second animal is.

Mathematical language

The language of ordinality relates naturally to the keys and animals of this story:

First key, first animal, gorilla;
Second key, second animal, elephant;
Third key, third animal, hyena;
Fourth key, fourth animal, lion;
Fifth key, fifth animal, giraffe;
Sixth key, sixth animal, armadillo.
The word 'armadillo' is supported with a picture image.

(McGrath 2013)

Puppets and props scaffold confidence

For the novice oral mathematical storyteller confidence is important: for some storytellers prop and puppets offer confidence, which is a valuable purpose. Rebecca tells me that the 'prop was a very big comfort blanket' (Belsten 2013b). In an honest reflection, Rebecca describes her belief that children would be more interested in the props than they would be in her as a nervous storyteller (Belsten 2013b). Rebecca and Rachel agree that as confidence grows props can be relied on less and stories retold without supporting materials (Adcock 2013b; Belsten 2013b).

Removing the prop or puppet scaffolding

It is worth reminding ourselves that the story can be told with or without prop or puppet: some storytellers choose not to include a prop. It is important not to over rely on the prop: subsequent story retellings can rely less on the scaffold of a prop. Puppet and props scaffold both teller and listener. Removal of a story scaffold requires children to imagine mathematical ideas. Scaffolding can be removed gradually as confidence in telling the story is established and as mathematical ideas become more secure.

Purpose

Props or puppets need to serve a purpose as part of the oral mathematical story otherwise they become an unnecessary distraction. Brown (2013c) describes a telling of Jack and the Bean Stalk with too many props, the experience becoming more like a 'play'. Wye (2013a) makes the point that the prop or puppet needs to extend the story experience. When she tells the story about the tiger Augustus (Rayner 2008), who lost his smile, she unwraps a mirror and each person listening to this story looks in the mirror and smiles (Wye 2013b). This captures the abstract idea of the tiger finding his smile. Props or puppets need to help children tune in to the abstract nature of oral story and mathematical ideas, in a purposeful way.

Range of puppets or props

Props or puppets range from story characters to objects that represent something about the story. Puppets or props can be original creations such as a shoemaker, elves, shoes; the gorilla hand puppet; Little Lumpty or items selected by the stoyteller. A prop can be both the story character and have features that make mathematical ideas explicit: for the story 'Ladybird on a Leaf' the prop is the story character and her spots support mathematical ideas (see Figure 8.4). Props can be chosen symbolic representations, such as a brass pot for the story 'Two of Everything' (Toy Hong 1993), where the pot has magical powers to double. Essentially the puppet or prop supports the oral story in a purposeful way, rather than distract from the business of oral mathematical story telling.

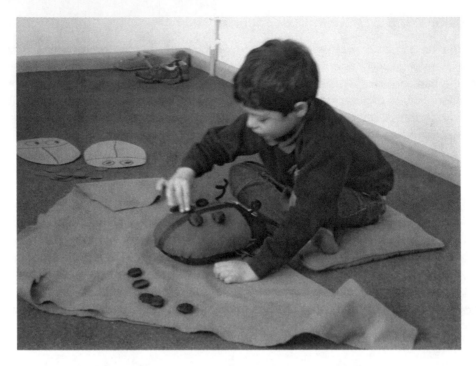

Figure 8.4 Daniel retells 'Ladybird on a Leaf' using the prop as a story character and the spots as concrete representations of his mathematical ideas

Puppets and props provide:

- mathematical motivation as they offer children a meaningful context to think about mathematical ideas
- concrete expression of otherwise abstract mathematical ideas: tangerines physically represent subtraction complements ($5 - 2 = 3$; $5 - 3 = 2$); spots on the back of the ladybird show the number relationship pattern ($5 - 2 + 2 = 5$)
- confidence for the storyteller. It might be that retellings are without the use of puppets or props as confidence grows.

Puppets and props are mathematical stories themselves

There is creative mathematical thinking in making puppets and props. One afternoon I tell the story 'Little Lumpty' to Early Childhood Studies students and show the design detail of his hat, body and shoes. I point out how detail of Lumpty's design relates to the story theme of counting in twos. I explain the idea of prop connecting children, story and mathematical idea: in one storytelling Lumpty counts in twos forwards and backwards as he climbs up and down the ladder.

Design detail: Little Lumpty character prop supports retelling of 'Little Lumpty' (Imai 1994)

Little Lumpty's design is based on multiples of two: holes on his shoes (2, 4, 6, 8, 10); sections of his hat (two red, two blue, two red, two blue), and four sections of his body (all white). Children are captivated by the 'Little Lumpty' prop, are motivated to count to the twelfth multiple of two, though it is beyond what they are familiar with, and are interested in hearing about how he was made (see Figure 8.5).

Little Lumpty tells a story of counting in multiples of two, a mathematical idea that also features in his design. There are two stories: what Little Lumpty does and how Little Lumpty is designed.

Foundation degree students are set a very open challenge: to prepare an oral story with mathematical intention; to create a prop or puppet to support the story if a prop will add to the story experience. Before the challenge leaves my lips I sense some students think of possibilities. Before I order materials Rebecca has made a world of elves and shoes, which inspires others. I am struck year on year by how hungry students are for creative opportunity.

Figure 8.5 A child looking at Little Lumpty's design.

Creative mathematical thinking

There is multiplicity of purpose in my request for students to create a supporting prop for an oral mathematical story. Students gain insight into the mathematical thinking involved in this creative process: they experience creative mathematical thinking. Moving from my abstract suggestion to a concrete representation requires students to engage in problem posing, problem solving and possibility thinking. Students create a problem of their own design, set about realising this design creation, solving unexpected problems before arriving at a satisfying solution. There is a combination of explicit and implicit mathematical thinking: creative and practical mathematical application.

I suggest that students provide a guide to making the prop or puppet as this encourages a strategic view, prompts an articulation of the process and provides a tool to tell the story of prop creation. When Rebecca brings the story of 'The Elves and the Shoemaker' to a Reception class, children ask her to tell how she made the shoemaker, elves and shoes. Rita asks Rebecca: 'How did you make the shoemakers hard and soft?' (see Figures 8.6 and 8.7).

Rebecca tells me she is glad she made the guide so that she can recall this creative process, confirming that it is a tool to explain to others. This guide involves proposing a problem for others to solve, which takes problem thinking to a higher level (McGrath 2010). I am interested to find out more about these students' choice of puppet or prop, their creation of the oral story with prop or puppet and their thoughts on taking their oral mathematical stories to children.

Figure 8.6 Children holding Rebecca's shoemaker props and asking how they were made.

Mathematics in making props or puppets: the story of shoemaker, elves and shoes

When making the shoes, Rebecca thinks of mathematics as the wellington boots are taller than the other shoes. Such design thinking keeps future mathematical discussion open to possibilities. Rebecca considers that there is scope to use these props across the curriculum.

Rachel explains a problem she encounters when making the hand puppet. She sews the two black body sections together, inverting these before realising she needs to sew on the face. The face should be sewn on before sewing the front and back panels together. On finishing, she realises her gorilla does not have ears, which could be misinterpreted as a design fault, but she advises she was following the image of the picture book (Rathmann 2012); this gorilla doesn't listen!

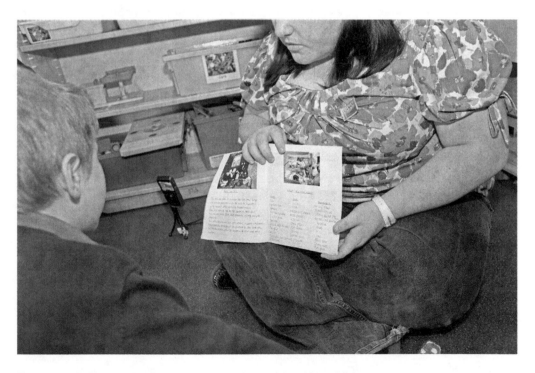

Figure 8.7 Rebecca sharing her prop making guide with a child.

Mathematics in making the gorilla hand puppet to support retelling of 'Goodnight Gorilla' (Rathmann 2012)

Retold by Rachel Adcock

The story of a hand puppet: Rachel wants to engage children by having a hand puppet representation of the main character. She particularly wants a hand puppet as children can easily put this on and take it off.

Creative mathematical thinking (moving from abstract suggestion): Rachel has the idea of representing a gorilla as a hand puppet.

Practical mathematical thinking (moving to practical application): she copies the image of the character represented in the picture book. She cuts out, matching front and back panels, she stitches the two, measuring thread. The front and back sections need careful alignment.

Unexpected problems (trial and error): Rachel realises after stitching front to back panel sections that the face has not been sewn on. She has to sew on and stuff the face, with the body of the puppet on her hand, trying not to prick herself.

Documenting the process (a tool to tell the puppet story): taking photographs of different stages of making props or puppet breaks the process down into steps that show a logical sequence. This helps the creator recall later what they did, and is a tool to tell the story of how the puppet or prop is made (see Appendix 6 for copy of guide).

Props and puppets nourish relationships between children, mathematical stories and storytellers

Nourishing creativity is important for the motivation and confidence of the novice oral mathematical storyteller. While the prop maker is posing and solving problems in making the prop, they arrive at a heightened motivation about their story. A relationship forges between storyteller, prop and story, which nourishes the creator.

The sharing of puppet making experiences with children provides insight into creative problem posing, and problem solving from an adult perspective. Children use practical mathematics without necessarily articulating it when they make robots, models and train tracks (McGrath 2010), and these accounts about how puppets and props are made tell stories about creative and practical application of mathematics by an adult. Children are fascinated to hear Rebecca's design story of how shoemaker, elves and shoes come to life.

Conclusion

Puppets and props are concrete representations of abstract features of story. The prop or puppet can be a character that children relate to and through which story context is made meaningful. As well as characterisation, puppets and props can connect story and mathematical abstractions in other ways: making mathematical ideas visual.

Puppets and props should support, scaffold and extend a mathematical story experience. A professional storyteller advises against including a prop unless it extends story experience. When Cassandra Wye tells the story of 'Augustus: The tiger who lost his smile' a mirror is unwrapped at the end and each listener looks at their smile, deepening this story experience. Puppets or props need to be used in a purposeful way; the mirror supports the abstract idea of a tiger finding his smile.

Making puppets and props involves creative mathematical thinking. The puppet maker moves from an abstract idea to a concrete outcome. There is possibility thinking as the features of the puppet are imagined. An original creative problem is posed in the maker's mind. Problem solving is exercised as the puppet comes to life. Unexpected problems present along the way: the face of the gorilla is difficult to sew on. Trial and error features as part of the design process, which is a problem solving strategy.

Creative mathematics is explicit in the design and implicit in puppet and prop making: there is creative thinking of possibilities and then practical measuring while making the props or puppets. Documenting a puppet making guide for others to follow serves to sharpen the mind as to what this involves. A guide to how the prop or puppet is made defines this creative experience, framing explicit and implicit mathematical thinking. The maker is well placed to tell the story about the mathematics involved in the making of props or puppets after recording the story in a guide and, as such, guides can be used as tools to share with children.

Props and puppets connect children to oral mathematical story experiences. Puppets or props support the abstract nature of the mathematical oral story experience. The purposes of puppets and props are multiple: motivating children's mathematical thinking; supporting visualisation of abstract mathematical ideas; and offering confidence to storytellers. The next chapter considers how children use story related puppets and props to retell oral mathematical stories.

9 | Children as mathematical storytellers

The Tempest (1611) act 5, sc. 1

Where the bee sucks, there suck I
In a cowslip's bell I lie;
There I couch when owls do cry.
On the bat's back I do fly
After summer merrily:
Merrily, merrily shall I live now
Under the blossom that hangs on the bough.

(Shakespeare 2009)

The aims of this chapter are to consider:

- an example of a child retelling a mathematical story with precision and imagination
- how oral story telling challenges children
- children playing with story and mathematical ideas as storytellers.

◀)) 'Penguin'

Told by Suzanne Kelham

Once upon a time there was a little penguin. His mum said to him:

'Go to the magical pond and catch ten fish for our tea.'
He walked a bit, and he walked a bit, and he walked a bit, and he walked a bit, until he got to the magical pond that glistens and shines.
'Today we have orange and lemon flavoured fish', the pond says.
Penguin fished, and fished and fished until he caught ten delicious fish for tea. But on bringing the catch home, the family eats the fish and is still hungry and so Penguin has to return to the pond with the lemon and orange flavours and find different ways to catch ten fish . . .

(Kelham 2013d)

Introduction

This chapter aims to describe what happens when children are given the opportunity to retell a mathematical story with props, and how, without prompting, children sometimes retell the story with remarkable *precision* and *imagination*.

Suzanne, a Reception class teacher, invites children to retell 'Penguin' with her. Children in a small group, presented with a flexible story idea, skillfully build up this story, keeping mathematical ideas intact. Following this story experience some children ask to be storytellers and one particular example of Freya retelling the story is described.

As with play, storytelling is something children can do with what could be misinterpreted as ease. Just as play is natural but hard work, so is navigating between storytelling and mathematical ideas. When children rise to the challenge as storytellers, they can extend ideas of stories heard to make different mathematical connections. Examples are discussed of children retelling stories in ways that extend mathematical ideas beyond that of a story heard.

This chapter describes examples that show how children who request to be storytellers pose themselves the challenge of retelling a story with mathematical content running through it to an audience, allowing their imagination to play with the story heard, using supporting props to recreate a mathematical story. Oral mathematical storytelling challenges children to solve problems of restructuring, reshaping and retelling a story. By asking to sit on the storyteller cushion, children set themselves challenges that we as adults can find difficult.

Children retelling mathematical stories with precision and imagination

Development of mathematical understanding involves building up connections in the mind of the listener. Oral mathematical story is an imaginative way of building mathematical connections: 'the more connections, the more secure and the more useful the understanding' (Haylock & Cockburn 2013, p.11). Making connections is a key process in learning mathematics (Haylock & Cockburn 2013; Suggate *et al.* 2010; 2006). Children connect many mathematical ideas when building stories, through creating story context, words, props, story maps and actions. Story props can be closely or loosely related to the story and in order to establish connections children need to move between auditory, visual and physical representations, which they can do as storytellers.

Children rebuild the story of 'Penguin' as a group

Suzanne invites children (aged four and five), most of whom have heard this story once, to rebuild a mathematical story about Penguin, who returns to the magical pond many times to discover different ways of making ten fish using lemon and orange flavours. Suzanne is flexible in facilitating children's mathematical ideas, allowing children to decide on the combination of fish Penguin catches. What I observe is very much a case of giving children the bare bones of a story idea and inviting them to rebuild the story through a series of repeated sequences using their own particular mathematical examples. Suzanne does not make any number complement suggestions but instead prompts children to work through possibilities. Where children suggest 'seven orange flavoured and three lemon flavoured' she prompts them to map this out using fish on the carpet (see Figure 9.1). When children suggest 'four orange and six lemon flavoured fish' Suzanne prompts children to think of 'six orange flavoured and four lemon flavoured fish', but without providing the answer. Suzanne makes a connection to other classroom learning when she asks children to think of numbers 'who love each other', another way of thinking of number complements.

By prompting children to play with the options, they start suggesting that there could be 'seven orange flavoured and three lemon flavoured or seven lemon flavoured and three orange flavoured fish'. Number complements for ten come through in the mathematical dialogue that features as part of this interactive story where children

Figure 9.1 Fish patterns on the carpet as part of children retelling 'Penguin'.

make the suggestions and their teacher prompts for more ideas by reconnecting children to the story sequence. These number relationships are set out on the carpet by the children, using the coloured fish. Ensuring there is a well-stocked supply of fish means children can keep the number complements they think of on the carpet whilst building new ones, which allows connections to be made to previous examples and prompts new possibilities.

Pattern

The children add another dimension to seeking number bonds or complements by changing the way they arrange the coloured fish. They superimpose another mathematical idea about pattern by not always placing all same-coloured fish together. Austen has a moment of realisation as he is guided to see different arrangements for seven and three. He carefully sets out (in this order) five lemon, two orange, two lemon and one orange fish, to make ten. He has to work hard to answer the question as to how many lemon and how many orange make ten for the story character Penguin. He realises that his pattern can be interpreted in the same way as another previously arranged pattern on the carpet if he adds his lemon and orange fish before thinking about the total number:

Austen's pattern of fish on the carpet

5 lemon + 2 orange + 2 lemon + 1 orange = 7 lemon + 3 orange = 10

$5 + 2 + 2 + 1 = 7 + 3 = 10$

Austen's seven lemon and three orange is the same as another child's but different in how he has set it out. His seven lemon fish is made up of a five and a two; his three orange is made up of a two and a one. Austen and other children start to make connections between the pattern arrangements on the carpet.

The colour combinations of fish are suggested by children randomly but have been rearranged to offer order for the reader: $10 + 0 = 10$; $0 + 10 = 10$; $9 + 1 = 10$; $1 + 9 = 10$; $8 + 2 = 10$; $2 + 8 = 10$; $7 + 3 = 10$; $3 + 7 = 10$; $6 + 4 = 10$; $4 + 6 = 10$; $5 + 5 = 10$.

After hearing and working through these number relations there is a frenzy as children discover that if they fold paper and cut one fish shape out they have more than one depending on the number of paper folds. One child is delighted with her discovery that 'ten came out'. Another child who has folded her paper in four is asked how many will be cut out but says, 'I don't know', excited to find out.

Freya retells 'Penguin' with *precision* and *imagination*

After hearing 'Penguin' Freya retells the story using the coloured fish with remarkable precision (see Figure 9.2). There is a notable hush as children cut fish and participate in a legitimate peripheral way (Lave & Wenger 1991) as Freya tells her story over seven minutes. I am amazed how children concentrate for this additional stretch of time, which is beyond what would be expected for four and five year olds. Freya develops her version of the story, using two soft toys, 'Duck' and 'Goose', which she picks out of a nearby box. She creatively adapts the story to fit with different characters, extends the story to try the number complement idea for 11 rather than ten, and creates an imaginative end. Her class teacher, Suzanne, tells me that she is usually quiet in whole class teaching contexts. Suzanne and I are both astonished by Freya's retelling of 'Penguin'.

The following is a transcript of Freya retelling 'Penguin' using cut-out coloured fish. Freya's words are in italics. Non-italic comment is to guide the reader when Freya repeats her count or supports the storytelling with actions. Freya is five years and 11 months old.

Figure 9.2 Freya using fish to tell 'Penguin'.

🔊 **Freya retelling 'Penguin'**

Retold by Freya aged 5 years, 11 months

Transcript of audio recording combined with notes made at the time

Mathematical idea: number complements for ten and 11

Once upon a time there was a duck
And this duck said to a seal, 'My mum wants you to go and get some fish
from the pond, the magical pond which shines and glistens'
So he went to the pond and he jumped into the pond
And he caught two yellow fish
(Repeats this phrase)
Two yellow fish, and three pink fish, and four orange fish and one blue fish
So he counted them 1, 2, 3, 4, 5, 6, 7, 8, 9, 10
He had ten altogether
And then he picked them up
And he went back home to Goose
'Here's your ten lovely fish'
'But I'm still hungry'
So he went back to the pond
And he caught one pink fish and four blue fish and he caught three yellow
fish and he caught two orange fish
And he counted them 1, 2, 3, 4, 5, 6, 7, 8, 9, 10
And he picked them up counting them in his head
And he took them back to Goose
'But I'm still hungry' said Goose
So he went back to the glistening and shining pond
And he caught two orange fish and took them back and counted them and
took them back to Goose
'I'm still hungry'
So he went back to the pond
And he went back to Goose
And she said 'I want 11 fish this time'
So he went back to the glistening and shining pond
And he caught five orange fish and four yellow fish . . .
(Freya puts down five orange fish then four yellow, then one yellow then one
blue fish)
And five yellow fish and one blue fish
So he counted them 1, 2, 3, 4, 5, 6, 7, 8, 9, 10, 11
And he picked them up counting them
And he took them back to Goose
And they had a big meal
Then when Goose was full after they all had those fish
She thought 'I'm too full up. Maybe I should have said I wanted two more fish'

The End

Story-related props help children construct mathematical ideas. Freya works through number relationships, using the coloured fish to support her articulation of these number relationships. She counts the fish, and tells us that the story character counts them. She decides on a new number and works out a combination of five orange and five yellow and one blue to make 11 fish. Freya extends the idea of number complements to a more challenging number of her choice.

Summary of mathematical ideas expressed in Freya's 'Penguin' story

Numbers making 10: 2+3+4+1=10
Counting accurately 1, 2, 3, 4, 5, 6, 7, 8, 9, 10
Total quantity: 'He had ten altogether'
Numbers making 10: 1+4+3+2=10
Numbers making 11: 5+5+1=11
Counting accurately 1, 2, 3, 4, 5, 6, 7, 8, 9, 10, 11

Freya uses her knowledge of counting and adding to build up her story, which mirrors the story heard but she adapts to allow new ideas. She uses the cut-out coloured fish to support these mathematical ideas.

Freya's story carries much of the original story but also shows evidence of applying the idea of number complements to a different number. Freya retells her story in a similar way to Jake (Chapter 3) but requests to be a storyteller. There are close parallels between Jake and Freya's retellings: playing with the props as storytellers.

Freya uses the 'Penguin' story to make her own oral mathematical story. This abstract experience, which was supported with a prop, is remodelled but with her own choice of number and number relationships. Freya has internalised the idea of using different coloured fish to work out different number complements. She connects this mathematical idea of the story heard to her own retelling using coloured fish in a visually supportive way. There is remarkable precision in how she retells the story of Penguin, testing a different number complement possibility, combining story and mathematical ideas imaginatively, offering a twist at the end.

Further discussion about children as storytellers is available in a chapter titled 'Mathematical Storyteller Kings and Queens: An alternative pedagogical choice to facilitate mathematical thinking and understand children's mathematical capabilities' in McGrath (2014).

Oral storytelling is challenging for children

Just as playing is hard work for children, so is storytelling. Such creative expression of mathematical ideas can be considered as what Haylock & Cockburn (2013, p.285) refer to as 'hard thinking': children are using story narrative as ways of organising and internalising mathematical ideas. I return to recordings of children retelling stories and note the following about how children respond when they are sitting on the storyteller cushion after requesting to be mathematical storytellers:

'Teremok' adapted from a Russian tale

(versions of the story are available in Arnold 1994; Ransome 2003)

Anna (four years and eight months) takes the storyteller role but doesn't seem to know what to do. I expect her to know but she talks instead of her hair being electric when she removes her clips. Perhaps she is nervous. She starts with, 'Once upon a time there was a kitty cat'. She shows great excitement about discovering a Gromit dog in the collection of toys. Anna's story starts with, 'Along came . . .' but quickly arrives at 'The end' and she hands over to Toby. Anna is unsure of what to do as a storyteller. Toby (five years and two months) tells the story with enthusiasm using the repetitive phrase 'knock, knock, knock, who will answer when I knock?' and positional language each time he brings soft toy animals to the hut. Following Toby's retelling, Anna retells the story as if she has learnt something about storytelling from Toby. Anna's storytelling is strengthened by listening to Toby, which supports Anna in becoming stronger at retelling her 'Teremok' story. This is an example of how a more accurate assessment of capabilities can be arrived at by allowing children the opportunity to model the demonstrations of others (Vygotsky 1978).

(McGrath 2013)

'Ladybird on a Leaf'

Toby, who previously modeled storytelling for his peer, sits on the storyteller's cushion after requesting to retell 'Ladybird on a Leaf' and says: 'I don't know what story', and 'this is *hard*'. Toby provides insight into the variable nature of this role as storyteller describing it as 'hard'. Though previously storytelling seemed to be something Toby did without hesitating, on this occasion he finds the role challenging.

(McGrath 2013)

'Handa's Return Journey' is based on the original story 'Handa's Surprise' (Browne 1998) and is about what could happen as Handa returns home with tangerines in her basket.

'Handa's Return Journey'

Holly (five years) struggles to start so I offer her an opening sentence. She tells the rest of her story by herself, creating an original subtraction story. She starts with five tangerines and uses story ideas to reduce this number to zero. She imaginatively describes a monkey not taking any tangerines because he only eats bananas and a zebra thinking of taking two but changing his mind as this would be greedy. Holly thinks through the story structure so that it leads to an empty basket of fruit. It takes time for her ideas to form and take shape but she expresses the following mathematical ideas: $5 - 2 = 3$; $3 - 1 = 2$; $2 - 0 = 2$; $2 - 1 = 1$; $1 - 1 = 0$.

(McGrath 2013)

These accounts reveal how children do not always find storytelling easy. It is interesting to note how children respond on different occasions: confidence as a storyteller is inconsistent. Interestingly, Freya retells 'Penguin' again and it is not as striking as on the first telling transcribed above. Harry tells a version of the story using a world of additional props that he finds stored in the room. Though his story becomes complex he keeps the story idea about losing and replacing equivalent numbers of spots at the core. I note how on some occasions a child's desire to entertain their audience takes over and the story serves a different function: to shock and generate hysterical laughter.

Children playing with story and mathematical ideas as storytellers

Mathematical ideas connecting within a story

Children make connections between story and mathematics, abstract mathematical ideas and concrete story-related props, particular mathematical ideas (number relationships) and interconnected mathematical ideas (counting, adding and subtracting) as they retell mathematical stories. Mathematical ideas work together within a story and can be played with to prompt other possibilities. When Freya retells the 'Penguin' story she carefully works through particular examples that support number complement patterns. However, there are many mathematical ideas working together within Freya's story.

Freya is working mainly with the number '10' and is not able to automatically recall what the number complements are. She uses her knowledge of counting, and adding, to find ways of expressing number complements. Freya establishes the pattern of the story and is connecting many mathematical ideas together.

Freya uses many mathematical ideas as she works on retelling the 'Penguin' story:

Counting accurately with one to one correspondence 1, 2, 3, 4, 5, 6, 7, 8, 9, 10, 11

Addition complements for 10

Addition complements for 11

Pattern: arranging the fish in a patterned way. 11 is composed of five orange fish, five yellow fish and one blue fish: $5 + 5 + 1 = 11$

Mathematical connections within stories

Oral mathematical story involves establishing connections between mathematical ideas. I now provide examples of children playing with story and mathematical ideas, extending story and mathematical ideas beyond those of stories told by adults.

'Teremok'

When Paula Brown tells this story to a class of 30 four and five year olds, the animals arrive at the hut one by one. Toby plays with the idea of this story, bringing two rabbits at a time, two dogs and then four animals together rather than individually. He is changing something about this story and inadvertently posing the question, 'what if instead of animals arriving one by one, they arrive in twos or fours?' This idea connects to what appears to be his desire to fill the box quicker. The full capacity of the hut will be reached faster if more animals are added each time.

Extract from Toby's retelling of 'Teremok'

'There was a little dog called Gromit, and he was walking and walking, and walking and he bumped into something. He looked on top, to the side, to the other side, and to the back, and underneath. He wondered what's inside.

Knock, knock, knock, who will answer when I knock?

Two dogs walking together, looked in front, at the back, at the side, on top, underneath. Two rabbits walking along, bumped into the house. They looked in front, at the back, at the sides, at the other sides, underneath, they wondered. All four [animals remaining] came together. There's room for all of us.'

'Penguin'

Jessica (five years and five months) retells this story but her story is about providing two piles of fish. She gets a story listener to check each pile. Jessica plays with the original story, introducing a character, to facilitate a mathematical idea about dividing a pile of fish from the pond into equal shares of fish. Another child, Lexie, adapts the 'Penguin' story to a different mathematical idea, adding 3 + 4 + 10 + 11 fish, playing with the story in a way that draws out a different mathematical idea: adding.

'Little Lumpty'

Mya (four years and 11 months) retells a lovely version of 'Little Lumpty' using a ladder with the prop character (see Figure 9.3). She decides Lumpty counts in multiples of five: '5, 10, 15, 30, 35, 40, 45, 50, 55, 60, 65' (note her mathematical error as there is no 20 or 25). In this retelling, Lumpty jumps off the wall and lands on a sheet. He leaves the ladder propped against the wall and returns to collect it and sleep on it.

Figure 9.3 Mya holds Little Lumpty ready to tell a story, which involves him counting in multiples of five to steady his nerves as he climbs a ladder.

The next day, Lumpty climbs another wall counting in multiples of five but this time to 70. Mya expresses the idea of finding the height of walls and looks for the 'tallest wall in town'; she decides the ladder is not long enough, so tries another wall. When Lumpty is on top of this wall, a neighbour takes back their ladder, leaving Lumpty stuck on top of the wall shouting, 'how am I going to get down?'

◀)) **'Little Lumpty'**

Retold by Anna aged 5 years, 2 months

Anna retells 'Little Lumpty' counting forwards in ones to 12; backwards in ones from 12, carefully placing Lumpty's foot on each rung of the ladder for each count (see Figure 9.4). She locates a bigger wall and Lumpty counts in twos to 24. Anna suggests counting in threes but declines this idea, instead counting in 'zoomy numbers'.

(adapted from Imai 1994)

Figure 9.4 Anna using Little Lumpty at the start of the count.

In each of the accounts outlined, children retell stories heard in ways that playfully connect mathematical and story ideas. They create stories that are rich in imaginative mathematical ideas. In the next account, Toby accidentally poses a question that could be used by adults to prompt mathematical thinking when retelling 'The Greedy Triangle' (Burns 1994).

'The Greedy Triangle'

In Chapter 7 we came upon an adapted version of this story about a shape witch who gives a triangle one corner and one side, so that the triangle becomes a square, then a pentagon, then a hexagon. The shape witch then takes away a corner and a side so that the hexagon becomes a pentagon, then a square before returning to be a triangle. Mathematical ideas about 2D shapes, addition and subtraction connect and work together through the context of this story (Burns 1994). In retelling 'The Greedy Triangle', Toby plays with the mathematical idea by chance.

Toby retells 'The Greedy Triangle' story

Toby selects shapes to use as supporting story props but there is no pentagon. The pentagon shape is not part of the available commercial collection of shapes. A cardboard version of the pentagon was made by his teacher Louise, for her telling of the shape story, but this pentagon seems to have disappeared! Toby retells the shape story and overcomes the lack of pentagon by chance, posing the idea of the shape witch giving the square two corners and two sides. In Toby's retelling the shape witch adds on two corners and two sides so the square becomes a hexagon, overcoming the need for a pentagon.

Within the one story many mathematical ideas connect together. One mathematical idea can be played with to change another: Toby plays with addition, needing to add on two rather than one corner and side, transforming a square into a hexagon, avoiding the need to represent a pentagon as there is none available for his retelling.

This idea of playing with the story so that the shape witch adds two sides and two corners connects to ideas put forward by children as part of the creative mathematical dialogue where a child poses the idea of turning the triangle into a circle, in Chapter 7. If the shape witch were to be very busy and add an infinite number of corners and sides, a triangle would become a circle. There is also an implication for our selection of story-related props: what would happen if a triangle, pentagon and septagon (a seven-sided shape) were provided?

Examples of children telling stories show how oral story and mathematical ideas connect to support creative mathematical thinking (Pound & Lee 2011). This experience relies on children extracting meaning from words and constructing mathematical ideas from these words to tell their mathematical story.

Conclusion

Children are remarkable in how they can retell a mathematical story with *precision* and *imagination* whilst extending to mathematical ideas that differ from those of the story told by adults. Freya retells 'Penguin' in a way that challenges her mathematical thinking and astonishes listening adults. In retelling stories, children play with story and mathematical ideas, finding ways to accommodate both.

Children reveal a flexible approach in retelling stories, opening out new mathematical possibilities, in natural and sometimes accidental ways. Story-related props allow children to do this. In 'Penguin' the supporting props are coloured fish, allowing much in the way of determining number relations and pattern. In retelling 'Little Lumpty', a ladder prompts children's counting in ones, twos and fives. The possibility of counting in threes is identified by a child, and could be something a listening adult decides to do, on retelling the story.

Children find the role of storyteller hard and though sometimes they may execute this role with remarkable skill it is important for adults not to hold a fixed expectation that this will always happen. A coherent, fluent, mathematically-sound oral story can happen but is not guaranteed. This is true for adults telling imaginative mathematical stories: it is important to have realistic expectations of children and of ourselves. Children as storytellers model peers and adults, allowing insightful assessment of their mathematical capabilities (Vygotsky 1978). The next chapter offers guidance on how to work through some of the challenges of oral mathematical storytelling, in order that as adults we can model for children.

10 Crafting and telling oral mathematical stories

Never Give In (1941)

Never give in, never give in
Never, never, never, never
In nothing great or small,
Large or petty–
Never give in.

(Churchill, 2005)

This chapter aims to gain insight into:

- educator and storyteller approaches to oral storytelling
- how storytellers craft and tell oral mathematical story
- challenges of oral mathematical storytelling.

'The Man Who Moved a Mountain'

In China there was a range of mountains that stretched all the way from one side of the country to the other. At the foot of one mountain was a house where a man and his wife and children lived. This family grew vegetables to sell at the market on the other side of the mountain. They had to walk a long way to get to the market and by the time they got there the vegetables would be bruised. The old man thought hard and decided that the best solution would be to move the mountain. Every day he filled a bucket with soil from the mountain and threw it into the sea. He did this day after day after day after day. A neighbour was puzzled and asked the man, 'What are you doing?' 'I am moving the mountain', the man replied. 'You will never move the mountain', the neighbour laughed. 'Maybe not in my lifetime, but in my children's, children's, children's, children's, lifetime', replied the man. And now if you go to China you will see a range of mountains stretching all the way from one side to the other but at one place there is a gap where a mountain might have been.

Adapted by Cassandra Wye (original story from The Book of Lieh-Tzu: A classic of Tao, 1990, translated by A.C. Graham)

Introduction

This chapter aims to elicit and offer guidance for some of the challenges of crafting and telling oral mathematical stories. Insights are drawn from watching story-tellers and educators who intentionally communicate mathematical ideas through story. For these individuals, storytelling with mathematical intent represents a new approach.

The essence of this chapter spans a range of contexts: I observe Cassandra Wye, a professional storyteller, share oral stories with children in assembly gatherings in several schools; I observe workshops that follow oral storytellings where children dramatise mathematical ideas of stories such as 'The Man Who Moved the Mountain'; I observe Cassandra train adults at conferences. Through these experiences I gain insight into how Cassandra as a professional storyteller steps into her storytelling zone, engaging with story, place and audience.

As part of the Early Childhood Studies foundation degree, Cassandra trains early years practitioners in the art of storytelling. Following training sessions, students adapt or create their own oral story, are video recorded telling stories to their peer group, analyse these videos and then reflect on skills prior to taking the story to children at early years settings. Kuyvenhoven (2009) advocates that storytelling should be included as part of initial training, acknowledging that it rarely is. Feedback at the end of the year from students reveals how this professional skill enriches confidence and enhances employability. A teaching assistant (Burns 2013a) excels at an interview for a new post, telling an oral story in a creative way, suggesting that this skill helps secure employment. Confidence grows through oral story work and skill as a mathematical storyteller is potentially a unique selling point for prospective employers.

Research supporting this book leads to working with another storyteller, Paula Brown. Paula has a less theatrical style compared to Cassandra. I observe Paula tell a story as part of the Bristol Storytelling Festival (Brown 2013d), to a group of 120 children aged between five and eight and to groups of 30 children aged four and five. Paula adapts the story 'Teremok', a Russian tale referred to in earlier chapters.

Educators keen to take a creative oral storytelling approach to teaching mathematics are video recorded and observed working with large and small groups of children. Videos prompt reflective discussions about the experience of oral math-ematical storytelling from a storyteller perspective. These observations illuminate what is involved in telling not just a good oral story, but a story with words that create mathematical images (Pound & Lee 2011); a story that helps children organise thoughts and think in mathematical detail (Walker 1975). Guidance about some of the challenges of oral mathematical storytelling are sketched out in this chapter.

Educator and storyteller approaches

Oral storytelling stokes the imagination. Allison (1987) describes how the spoken word holds power and mystery. Bryant (1947) describes how the oral storyteller is bound by nothing. Oral storytelling is arguably stronger in power of expression than reading, as mentioned in Chapter 2. Those who earn most of their living as storytellers are termed 'professional storytellers' (Wye 2013a). Educationalists can take something from professional storytellers: Suzanne (Reception class teacher) tells me that teachers can take some of what storytellers do to their professional lives (Kelham 2013b).

An oral mathematical story experience relies on the preparation of a story that is told with ease if the story is to help children conceptualise mathematical ideas. Telling a story is another way of establishing mathematical meaning. The story fixes a mathematical idea and potentially a pattern. The storyteller can create imaginative mathematical images and understandable explanations of abstract mathematical ideas (Kuyvenhoven 2009). The experience helps children structure mathematical thoughts. Through oral story children see the wonder that lies hidden within story and mathematics.

Crafting a mathematical story presents creative challenge. Challenge is differentiated depending on whether:

- an existing story with implicit or explicit mathematical ideas is retold. Cassandra Wye retells 'The Man Who Moved the Mountain', which expresses implicit mathematical ideas; workshops following the storytelling make these more explicit (Wye 2013c). This story connects to emotions associated with being a mathematician: stamina, persistence, pursuing a solution perceived by others as unrealistic, i.e. moving a mountain. Cassandra tells the story and afterwards invites children in the workshops to think of shapes of vegetables and ways of transporting vegetables beyond the mountain to the market. Children dramatise the weight of buckets filled with soil and patterns of movement as the man goes from the mountain to the sea.
- an original story is changed or adapted to make mathematics explicit. Paula Brown adapts the Russian tale 'Teremok', (other versions include, 'Knock, Knock, Teremok!', Arnold 1994; 'Who Lived in the Skull?', Ransome 2003), placing emphasis on positional language, sequencing and capacity (Brown 2013a). Suzanne and Louise, Reception class teachers, adapt the story 'The Greedy Triangle' (Burns 1994), putting emphasis on children mentally visualisng a triangle changing to a square, pentagon and hexagon and back to a pentagon, square and triangle. Kirsty Burns (2013b), a teaching assistant, adapts 'The Enormous Turnip' (Beck 2004) (Figure 10.1) to work with mathematical language of size. ◀))
- a story is created expressing an explicit mathematical idea. Suzanne, a Reception class teacher, creates stories such as 'Penguin', combining story and mathematical narrative in flexible ways.

Figure 10.1 Kirsty Burns sets up a room with props for telling 'The Enormous Turnip' with Reception class children.

How storytellers craft and tell oral mathematical story

Presented with the challenge of telling a story with mathematical emphasis, how do storytellers craft, tell and reflect on their stories?

Moment of connection

Preceding rare moments of connection (Hartman 2002), when everything comes together, is preparation. It is interesting to go behind the scenes and note what is involved. Cassandra describes the attention to detail that is important to the outcome of a positive story experience as a professional storyteller (Wye 2013a). There is work before the moment; gauging, adapting and adjusting in the moment (Hartman 2002; Parkinson 2011); and after there is work reflecting on the storytelling. When the preparation pays off it is similar to the moment of realising students are really with you in a lecture; an 'apple pie' moment when you are experiencing a lovely day out; a moment when a child says two and three is the same as three and two (2 + 3 = 3 + 2), or that words such as 'well' have many meanings.

The place

A place shapes or prevents the application of the story (Kuyvenhoven 2009). Where the story is told adds to or detracts from the story experience. I notice over the years that Cassandra arrives early to the college and spends time settling into the place. When I arrive with Cassandra at Torbay for a conference combining story and theoretical perspectives, I notice how she checks out locations allocated for workshops and negotiates changes as she assesses that some spaces won't work well for 50 delegates (McGrath 2012b). It is as if her presence primes the place for storytelling. *Where* children listen to a story is important. It is necessary to consider the space, how the chairs or cushions are arranged, the light, the acoustics, and to relocate if it is not conducive to a quality experience. Suzanne retells her 'Penguin' story in a different side room after finding the first telling is disturbed by noisy hand dryers in the toilets. Most locations will have limitations, but the point is to bother to find out what these are and whether you can work with them.

Hooks: starting sentence and repetitive phrases

I notice that, as the time to deliver approaches, Cassandra withdraws into herself and chants or hums a sound. It is an act of priming her mind, as if she charges herself up. I notice with students and educators a moment of anxiety just before starting a story, as if words might not form. After the first words, the storyteller falls into the stream of story, falling off the story ledge. I suggest having a well-formed first sentence, which I call a 'beginning hook' (Lipke 1996): for the 'Ladybird' story, 'once upon a leaf there was an old ladybird' gets me over the void of the first moment.

Repetitive phrase

Repetitive phrases consistent in structure serve as connections for children and storytellers (Allison 1987; Bryant 1947; Hartman 2002; Lipman 1999). The opening line and repetitive phrase are worth committing to memory. The rest of the story is best impressed as a sequence on the mind and not memorised line by line. A story map (Corbett 2007; 2006), diagram or notes can be referred to while telling the story.

Making mathematics explicit: a thinking string

I advocate sharing with children the bones of the mathematical intention before starting the story. Mathematical themes can be indicated before, during and after the story and as Hughes (1986) advises it is important not to be afraid of explicit teaching. I refer to a 'thinking string' connecting story and mathematics and return to this after telling stories, asking children about their thinking string: what ideas travel across their string? When I tell the story 'Little Lumpty' to a small group of children I write 'counting in multiples of two' on a small white board, and have bluetac on a string that I hold up to my head, explaining that I am joining this mathematical idea to a story from my head. Mya asks if she can retell the story and surprises me as she writes out 'counting in multiples of fives' on a white board (see also Chapter 9). Setting out the mathematical intention is something this child models (see Figure 10.2).

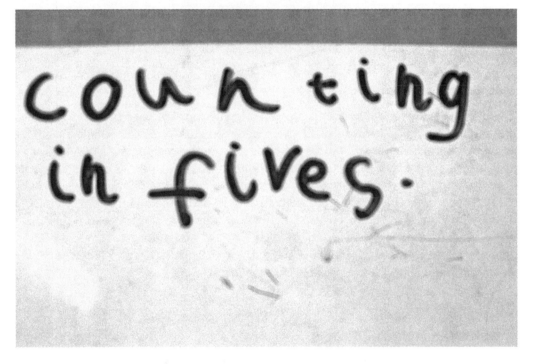

Figure 10.2 Mya writes out her mathematical idea for Little Lumpty 'counting in multiples of fives'.

Road map for mathematics

An oral mathematical story needs to be prepared with care: care of story narrative and care of mathematical ideas. Mathematical ideas need to be stripped down to bare bones and understood by the teller. A depth of mathematical understanding is important if the educator is to facilitate making connections with mathematical ideas.

With smaller groups there tends to be greater opportunity to play with the story and to play with the mathematics. To play with mathematical ideas there needs to be a grasp of what the mathematical idea is about. Without this it is easy to fall into confusion, misunderstanding, and to lose our way. Making connections and seeing patterns is like a road map for mathematics (Suggate *et al.* 2010; 2006). With a map we can negotiate direction; we need to have 'relational understanding' as well as 'instrumental understanding' (Skemp, cited in Suggate *et al.* 2010, p.7). To have relational understanding we need to know how the particulars of mathematics connect more generally (a map of where our destination is located in relation to where we are). The oral mathematical storyteller tells a mathematical story: to play with the mathematical direction there is a need to see patterns and mathematical possibilities beyond the story, to understand how the mathematical ideas of the story relate to other mathematical ideas.

Mathematical maps

The plot line is the road map for the story. A plot line runs between the story narrative and the mathematical ideas. A relationship between story and mathematics is set up in a way that allows the story to be changed so that the mathematics changes. The storyteller needs maps to signpost the structures of story and mathematical ideas. The challenge is to move between two maps: sequence of story and mathematical ideas. I recommend sketching out both story and mathematical maps, so that it is easier to navigate as a storyteller. Mathematical maps for addition and subtraction show how patterns can be established as part of storytellings: 'Handa's Return Journey' is an oral story based on the original story 'Handa's Surprise' (Browne 1998), which can be playfully told to prompt mathematical ideas.

'Handa's Return Journey'

When Handa sets off on a return journey from Akeyo's village with five tangerines in her basket, a monkey at first takes three tangerines, decides this is too greedy as it leaves only two in the basket, replaces three and then runs off with two tangerines. When Handa arrives at her village she lowers her basket to find three tangerines, unless of course something else happens . . .

Mathematical map: if $c = a + b$ then $c - a = b$ and $c - b = a$.

Particular example: if $5 = 3 + 2$ then $5 - 3 = 2$ and $5 - 2 = 3$.

'Ladybird on a Leaf'

The old ladybird checks the weather forecast and attaches five artificial spots in anticipation of her friend arriving early. A cheeky rain cloud passes over and washes two spots away saying, 'What's gone is gone!' but the friendly ant, who knows that the ladybird is embarrassed because she has no natural spots, sees this and, without the ladybird knowing, sticks the two spots back on saying, 'What's on is on'. Alternatively, the ant might feel mischievous and stick three spots onto the ladybird's back: perhaps the rain cloud notices the ant's trick and washes these three spots off.

Mathematical maps: $N - n + n = N$; and $N + n - n = N$.

Particular example: $5 - 2 + 2 = 5$; and $5 + 3 - 3 = 5$.

Children seeing mathematical ideas through story narrative

A good narrative extends to imaging and questioning (Haynes & Murris 2012). However, Haynes and Murris (2012) caution about interpreting how children make sense of what is communicated. Sometimes children see mathematical ideas differently but not necessarily incorrectly. Ikran for example sees a ladybird with five spots, three on one wing and two on the other. When one spot is washed away by rain she sees this as $3 - 1 = 2$ rather than $5 - 1 = 4$, describing the change to spots on one of the ladybird wings rather than the body as a whole. Children sometimes give an answer that is correct if seen from a certain perspective.

Storytellers as mathematical beings

Crafting an oral mathematical story draws on our creativity as a creator of story but also on our mathematical being (Mason 1989). Storytellers need to understand mathematics from children's perspectives: 'engaging seriously with the structure of mathematical ideas in terms of how children come to understand them is often the way in which teachers' own understanding of the mathematics they teach is enhanced and strengthened' (Haylock & Cockburn 2013, p.7). Our mathematical state of being can be fine-tuned by reading books that delve into the essence of mathematical ideas. I suggest a small stock of books that express accessible ideas about teaching mathematics (see references in text and list at end).

Challenges of oral mathematical storytelling

In creating an oral mathematical story a relationship between story and mathematics is established: story and mathematics become companions. There are challenges in managing this companionship: challenges that deepen if the story allows children to make mathematical generalisations such as 'N + n − n = N or N − n + n = N', which in words translates as a number always remains unchanged if the number added and then subtracted from it is the same; or, a number always remains unchanged if the number subtracted and then added to it is the same. One of the challenges as a storyteller is managing the relationship between the story and the mathematics to allow children a sense of this pattern.

Managing story and mathematical relationships

Oral story is potentially a creative mathematical experience. There can be tensions inherent in how the storyteller manages this experience. Haylock and Cockburn (2013) consider creativity in mathematics as children thinking flexibly; the challenge for the storyteller is to funnel this creativity in a way that leads children to make mathematical connections. We want children to connect the story and particular mathematical ideas of the story and then describe mathematical patterns. There is a balance to be struck between creative oral story narrative and creative mathematical insight: if the story narrative dominates, the mathematical idea might not happen; if mathematics overpowers, the story is diminished and the experience becomes something else.

Managing props and story

Louise Cheshire, a Reception class teacher, tells a story using hats and sticks as props to support mathematical ideas of doubling and halving. Immediately after the story she makes a point about how it is difficult to strike a balance between keeping the story going and using the props to make mathematical ideas explicit. When Louise retells this story reducing the props children struggle to visualise doubling of three sticks to six. The need to manage the relationship between story and props, along with the importance of props to make the mathematical ideas visual for young children, is important to consider. Retellings of the same story may allow for props to be used less as ideas become more secure.

Careful crafting of story and mathematics

Being able to see patterns, make connections and state generalisations liberates us from working out each case. As well as mathematical facts and concepts, mathematics is also about reasoning, which children need to exercise (Haylock & Cockburn, 2013). If we can see the pattern, we don't have to tediously work through the fine detail. If we see that $a + b = b + a$, we more readily see that $2 + 3 = 5$ will mean that $3 + 2 = 5$

without needing to work it out. Being able to generalise liberates children from needing to work through particular examples. The possibility of achieving this through a mathematical oral story can be realised, but depends on careful crafting of story and mathematical idea.

Making adjustments when ideas are not working

I tell 'Ladybird on a Leaf' several times before managing to bite into what it can really achieve. I manage many number relationships before working the story in a way that leads children to articulate the pattern: $N + n - n = N$ or $N - n + n = N$. I now explain through reflection some of the changes I made. First, I return to the idea of generalisations, which are statements with reference to something that is always the case (Haylock & Cockburn 2013, p.297). Haylock and Cockburn (2013, p.297) offer an example: 'If you add 6 to a number and then subtract 6 from the answer you always get back to the number you started with', which corresponds to the ladybird story pattern $N + 6 - 6 = N$. For 'Ladybird on a Leaf', if you add six spots to a number, say five, and then subtract six from the answer you always get back the number you started with, five: expressed numerically $5 + 6 - 6 = 5$.

I repeat the pattern $N + n - n = N$ several times, allowing children to decide on the 'N' and the 'n' numbers. When children are invited to explain to the ladybird what is going on, they articulate the pattern using very general story terms: 'The ant puts spots on and the rain washes spots away'.

I reflect that there is too much going on in my story. Because the N number keeps changing, it is more difficult to see the patterns $N - n + n = N$ or $N + n - n = N$. The number 'N' needs to remain constant so that children will see that adding and subtracting the same number of spots will not change the ladybird's appearance.

Reflections on telling 'Ladybird on a Leaf'

When I tell the ladybird subtraction story where 'N' (the number of spots worn) varies, a child can say the ant adds spots and the rain washes the same number away. But until I strip the mathematics down and structure the story so that N stays the same, the pattern $N+n-n=N$ goes unnoticed. Before this the only pattern the children could see was that the ant added spots on and the rain removes spots, which is a generalisation, but leaves me disappointed as it doesn't express fully the intended mathematical idea. I need to fine tune the relationship between the story and the mathematics, so that the emphasis is on the original number of spots remaining the same.

(McGrath 2013)

To refine, I fix the original 'N' and only allow 'n', the number of spots added by the ant and washed away by the rain, to change. The pattern is then clearer and speaks louder, particularly if the ant is always first and the rain follows.

Mathematical map

Mathematical pattern: $N + n - n = N$

Fixing the original number 'N': if 'N' is 5, possibilities with a total stock of ten spots include $5 + 5 - 5 = 5$; $5 + 4 - 4 = 5$; $5 + 3 - 3 = 5$; $5 + 2 - 2 = 5$; $5 + 1 - 1 = 5$; $5 + 0 - 0 = 5$.

Framing the question as, 'what if the ladybird has five spots, but the ant adds on different numbers of spots which the rain washes away?' fixes the mathematics in my mind, which leads children to generalise the pattern more precisely: when the rain removes three spots, a child directs me to 'tell the ant to put three back on', which, though relating to a particular example, shows a sense that he knows how this pattern works.

I also realise that the number of spots available determines where the story and mathematical pattern can go. If the weather is sunny, the ladybird could risk wearing ten spots, which determines the story idea of the rain removing spots before the ant puts them back, if the total number of spots available is ten. The story must go first in the rain direction if all the spots are worn to start ($N - n + n = N$); more spots would be required if the pattern $N + n - n = N$ were to be followed.

Resolution

As an oral mathematical storyteller I need to get under the skin of my story. I need to be at the core: the core of story and at the core of mathematical ideas. The adult is in a place of play (Hartman 2002): story play and mathematical play. After some time I resolve the problem in the story in a way that allows children to explain the mathematical pattern of the story very generally. There are relationships to manage between the storyteller, the listener, the story, the particular mathematical ideas of the story and beyond the story.

Resolution between each of the variables described brings the storyteller to that rare moment when a child makes mathematical connections through the oral story experience. Relationships need to be resolved and to move along a spectrum, depending on the story situation and the storyteller's connection to mathematics, story and audience. This is challenging and more complex than reading stories to children. Suzanne, a class teacher who takes on the challenge of oral mathematical storytelling with Reception class children, reflects on the nature of oral mathematical storytelling experience: 'When I have done any storytelling in the past it has been storyteller/ storylisteners. This has helped me realise that [oral mathematical storytelling] is a living interactive relational experience which is creative, exciting and unknown.'

Conclusion

This chapter tells the story of storytellers who tell stories for a living and adults who teach for a living. Stories are told by storytellers and educators with mathematical intention, using techniques and styles unique to the teller. Educationists move between adapting published stories and creating original stories to contextualise mathematical ideas.

To arrive at that moment of connection between story, child and teller there is an inter-play of skills, techniques and preparation. Storytellers place themselves inside the stories. Oral mathematical storytelling is about being inside the story and mathematical ideas. Storytellers need to question their relationship with mathematical ideas of the stories they tell.

Connections between story and mathematics can be made on different levels. However, to project particular mathematical ideas to a more general pattern in an explicit way requires deep mathematical knowledge. This is not to say a storyteller cannot achieve this, but rather to make the point that firming up on mathematical insight opens out possibilities to project the particular mathematical idea to a bigger pattern, so that children can make mathematical connections, see patterns, and generalise beyond the particular, leading to 'relational understanding' (Skemp, cited in Suggate *et al.* 2010; 2006). If children are to make mathematical generalisations, the storyteller needs to be inside the mathematics and the story, realising what to fix and what to free.

Conclusion

Please may I have a turn?

Toby asking to take a place on the storyteller cushion

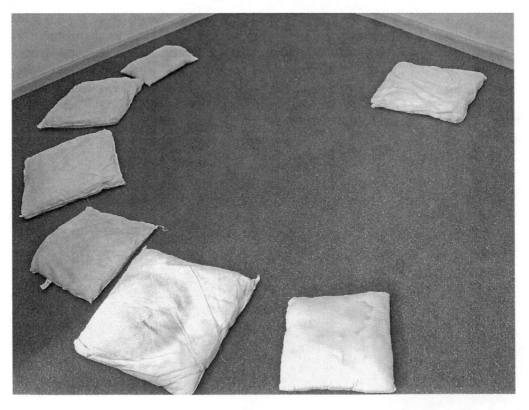

Figure C.1 Collection of six cushions inviting small group oral mathematical storytelling.

When children are in oral story environments they problematise mathematical ideas through the story context. Children use the story idea to try out mathematical concepts beyond what they hear in the stories told by adults; they connect the story heard to new mathematical relationships. Children are precise, articulate, natural tellers of stories with mathematical ideas but can find the role as storyteller challenging.

As shown by the research project, children are eager to tell mathematical stories using props and puppets that they see adults use to make mathematical ideas explicit. The ritual of oral mathematical storytelling as an outcome of the research project quickly becomes established: children sit on cushions arranged in a semicircle, often taking off their shoes, negotiating roles as storyteller or listener and drawing or cutting while they listen or tell stories over extended time spans.

Possibilities

This book explores the possibility of using published story and oral story as ways of facilitating children's mathematical engagement drawing on the findings of a research project. These mathematical experiences can be based on published texts or can be original imaginative story creations.

The main goal of the project was to investigate whether and how story and mathematics can work together to elicit mathematical activity in children. To gather understanding about this pedagogical approach, children (aged between four and seven years), storytellers and educators were observed, video recorded, photographed and audio recorded while listening to, constructing and playing with props and taking the role of storytellers. Children's overt responses to stories tell something about their engagement with mathematical ideas in the fabric of these stories.

Children as oral mathematical storytellers

Children will not always express mathematical ideas of story in play, but when children decide to model the role of storyteller and 'play' in this context they often express the story and the mathematical ideas explicitly. As storytellers, children play with story props with a motive to recreate a mathematical story. Children show willingness to be oral mathematical storytellers unprompted by adults. Something fascinating happens when children take the role of storyteller and create oral mathematical stories that other children listen to willingly as legitimate peripheral participants (Lave & Wenger 1991).

Despite the challenge, children can be natural storytellers, but the surprise is how skilled they also can be as natural oral mathematical storytellers. Freya retells 'Penguin', cutting her story pattern with remarkable precision, keeping the story structure intact and yet pressing on a new mathematical idea. This happens often enough with other children to persuade me that this desire should be encouraged.

139

Children classified as lower ability, children acquiring English as a second language and children showing autistic characteristics, respond favourably to oral story experiences created over the course of this project. However, it needs to be noted that oral story does not always work in the same way, and though sometimes it is possible to identify the snags, other times they remain elusive. Oral story is not the saviour of mathematics (Pound & Lee 2011; Schiro 2004) but offers a creative alternative to complement other pedagogical approaches. As Suzanne concludes after her experience facilitating children's mathematical thinking through oral story: 'When I first began working on this project I would get really anxious about the storytelling. Now I feel confident about adapting and creating my own stories and feel I will use this approach to introduce mathematical concepts.' As an approach it can be used alongside others to introduce or develop mathematical ideas with young children.

Oral mathematical story experiences encourage children to solve problems creatively and in ways that can require communication using words, actions and physical representations of ideas with story-related materials. Moments of connection, when children realise something about a mathematical idea, don't always happen, but when they do you know it!

Oral mathematical story offers adults the possibility of growing in confidence and being surprised by how some children respond to these experiences. Suzanne Kelham, the Reception class teacher who contributes to the project, offers the following reflections on her experience:

> I have grown in confidence, from a teacher who stuck to traditional tales, to being able to create my own stories based on mathematical concepts, confidently telling them with just a simple story map as a prompt. I have also realised that I have underestimated some children – being surprised by the storytelling confidence displayed by children such as Freya who are very quiet in whole class storytelling.

Key ideas

Problem posing and problem solving are like wheels that turn mathematics, story and play. The conjectural question of 'what if?' is like a key opening out new mathematical, story and play possibilities. Story holds abstract mathematical and story ideas in contexts that engage children.

Story-related props and puppets serve a purpose of making abstract mathematical ideas explicit; they make particular mathematical ideas visual for children. We note several cases of children structuring number relationships through abstract story ideas with associated props. The spots on the back of the Ladybird make the number pattern $N - n + n = N$ or $N + n - n = N$ visual, and allow children such as Jake to work through what are, for him, challenging mathematical ideas such as $12 - 7 + 7 = 12$. The coloured fish allow Freya to construct several number complements, using pattern of colour.

There are three key themes binding story, mathematics and play together in a natural way:

1 Problem posing, problem solving and problem creating
2 Questioning: 'What if?'
3 Representing abstract ideas in a concrete way.

A story shared with children either as a picture book, printed text or an oral story with supporting props brings story, mathematics and play together in a creative way. Combining story and mathematics in a genuine way draws in problem posing, as most story characters have a problem to solve; meaning needs to be abstracted from words; and the question 'what if?' opens out new problems in a playful way. Mathematics and oral story share an abstract quality, which children relate to (Egan 1988). Children move between abstract ideas of story to concrete expression of mathematical ideas using story-related props, combining abstract and concrete skillfully when they retell stories.

Working with published and oral mathematical story

Props and puppets are tools to support and extend story experiences that can be selected rather than created, if preferred. They can loosely represent something about the story or be more closely connected in a way that enables visualisation of mathematical ideas. Young children need supporting props to help scaffold mathematical ideas. These can be as simple as sticks or stones, jar lids for cookies or as creative as the 'Gorilla' hand puppet and the 'Elves and the Shoemaker' props that foundation degree students made in Chapter 8.

In quality children's literature there is often an unintentional relationship between mathematics and story, which, as adults, we can make intentional. As part of this project, picture books of high literary quality are adapted for oral storytelling purposes. These unintentional mathematical ideas are made more explicit by framing the picture book with the learning-supportive characteristics identified by Van den Heuvel-Panhuizen and Elia (2012).

A story profile serves to break the structure into component parts so that we can understand how it works and find mathematical ideas. Children's mathematical behaviour can be captured using an observational tool drawing from a format proposed by Casey (2011; 1999) and an assessment format proposed by Carr (2001). Vygotsky (1978) held the view that it is not enough to assess what the child knows; rather, we should assess the knowledge of children who have been supported by adult demonstration. Through the story experiences described in this book, children model adults and peers as oral mathematical storytellers, revealing to observers their ability to think mathematically (Vygotsky 1978). This observational tool can be used when observing children partaking in storytelling sessions, playing or retelling oral mathematical stories in ways that allow children and parents to contribute. Audio recording and observation of story-related playing and storytelling gives insight into children's mathematical language and I recommend the use of dictaphones, as recordings of children retelling mathematical stories add a valuable dimension to work with young children, allowing us to understand oral story for what it is (Paley 1999, 1981; Parkinson 2011).

Tuning in to our mathematical beings

Making a map of connections between mathematical ideas helps storytellers prepare possibilities that can be prompted by asking children 'what if?' Breaking mathematics down into components is part of the skill of teaching (Haylock & Cockburn 2013). Getting under the skin of the story and mathematical ideas brings moments of connection when children make realisations, see patterns and make generalisations, becoming freer in their thinking. One way to get under the skin of mathematics is to bore down into mathematical ideas by reading books that communicate about mathematics in accessible ways. As storytellers it is wise to question our relationships with story and mathematics and tune in to our mathematical being (Mason 1989).

Tools to assist oral mathematical story work include:

- story profile
- identifying learning-supportive characteristics
- maps of story and maps of mathematical ideas
- observation record to capture children's mathematical behaviour.

Making mathematical ideas explicit

Making mathematical intentions explicit before, during and after oral storytelling, provides language that confirms the intention in the storyteller's mind and gives children words to explain what happens. Hughes (1986) advises against being afraid of explicit teaching: children articulating explicit aims of literacy teaching show a capacity for this. In one storytelling scenario, Mya decides on and writes out the mathematical phrase 'counting in multiples of five' using this idea in her storytelling. Providing the language of explicit mathematical ideas supports a child's explanation about what is happening mathematically: children use story language ('the rain is taking spots away but the ant puts them back on') and mathematical terms ('it's a pattern and each time you count you miss one'). Such articulations of mathematical ideas forces intuitive understanding (Fisher 2009; Schiro 2004). Making mathematical ideas explicit does not need to damage the story experience and offers children a way to construct mathematical explanations.

Different story experiences

Different story experiences are created depending on the number of children listening to a story. It is possible to have positive mathematical story experiences with larger groups but with smaller numbers it is easier to be alongside and to facilitate creative mathematical dialogue.

Flexible storytelling alongside children

One could start with a picture book and prompt a creative mathematical discussion. However, retelling a story without the picture book creates a very different story experience. After becoming familiar with the story plot, the story can be reconstructed with children inviting their story and mathematical ideas. 'What if?' is the key question to think of as a way of turning the story over to fall into a different shape. Suzanne creates her own story idea and connects this to number complements for ten. When she tells the story it is in a flexible way, playfully constructing the story of 'Penguin' with children contributing all of the mathematical ideas, responding to the question 'what if there is another way for Penguin to catch ten fish using the orange and lemon flavours?' Creative mathematical dialogue features naturally as part of flexible story experiences. Oral story encourages flexible thinking, which is an approach favoured for teaching mathematics (Haylock & Cockburn 2013; Stanford 2012).

Future

This book makes the connection between mathematics, literature and oral story. The meaningful context that literature offers is extended to oral story. Oral story allows flexibility, as story plot can be played with in a way that requires thinking about mathematical ideas. This book opens out a different pedagogical possibility but closes only some of the questions and uncertainties of this creative approach. There is much more to be explored: linking other stories and other mathematical ideas.

Oral story is a powerful way for children to engage flexibly and creatively with mathematics. There is a natural relationship between story, mathematics and play, which children and educators can enjoy. Through the project I observe children posing problems for themselves when they take the role of storyteller, solving these problems when they retell stories using supporting materials. Children's spontaneous imaginative mathematical ideas strike me as positive outcomes worth pursuing. Oral mathematical storytelling allows educators to be creative and find something out about themselves. It is a question of posing a creative problem, using trial and error as a strategy to solve it: try it, and like Augustus the tiger, find your smile!

Appendix 1

Mathematical observation tool

Mathematical observation

Mathematical features	Narrative description
Conjecturing: 'What if?' (problem posing)	
Algorithm (for example, adding, subtracting, multiplying, dividing)	
Mathematical utterances (mathematical words)	
Mathematical facts	
Generalisation (making mathematical connections, seeing patterns)	
Mathematical mistakes or misunderstandings	
Transferring mathematical ideas to play contexts	
Curiosity (within mathematical context)	
Fluency (ease of use of mathematical ideas)	

Title	Age of child in years and months	Gender	Context	Initials of observer	Date	Audio recorded reference

Prompts	Observer comments
Transfer of mathematical ideas to context such as play or retelling stories Use of props Connection to original story heard Extending ideas Follow up	

Outcome of discussion with child	Outcome of discussion with parent

Source: Carr 2001

Appendix 2

Story profile template

	Story profile
Place	
Character	
Consciousness of character	
Time (frame)	
Plot (problem)	
Point of view	

Events (sequence)	
Simple detail (connecting story and real world)	
Repetition (phrase)	
Opening line	
Mathematical possibilities: 'What if?'	

Appendix 3

Story profile: 'Handa's Surprise' by Eileen Browne

	Structure and summary of story
	'Handa's Surprise' by Eileen Browne
Place African village	Handa sets off with seven exotic fruits in a basket on her head for her friend Akeyo. One at a time each piece of fruit is taken by one of seven different animals:
Character Handa	Handa put seven delicious fruits in a basket for her friend, Akeyo. She will be surprised, thought Handa as she set off for Akeyo's village.
Consciousness of character Handa is unaware of what is happening above her head.	'I wonder which fruit she'll like best? Will she like the soft yellow banana . . . or the sweet-smelling guava?
Time (frame) Day time; interval is unspecified	Will she like the round juicy orange . . . or the ripe red mango?
Plot (problem) Seven animals take seven fruit leaving an empty basket which is accidentally refilled by a goat knocking into a tree. Handa and her friend Akeyo are surprised to find tangerines.	Will she like the spiky-leaved pineapple . . . the creamy green avocado . . . or the tangy purple passion fruit? Which fruit will Akeyo like best?' A tethered goat escapes and knocks into a tree, dropping tangerines into Handa's empty basket: 'Hello, Akeyo', said Handa. 'I've brought you a surprise.' 'Tangerines!' said Akeyo. 'My favourite fruit.' 'TANGERINES?' said Handa. 'That is a surprise!'
Point of view Reader	

Events (sequence)	Illustrations: Illustrations show a monkey, ostrich, zebra, elephant, giraffe, antelope and parrot taking the fruit piece by piece. The idea of perspective (positional language), and that one cannot see what is happening above one's head when looking straight ahead, is conveyed in the pictures. The story of what happens to the fruit is carried in the pictures.
Handa fills the basket with seven fruits. Seven animals take one fruit each. The basket is filled with tangerines as a goat knocks into a tree. Handa arrives at Akeyo's village and lowers the basket to find tangerines.	**Relationship between story and mathematics:** The story is simple. It's a journey with the idea that when carrying something on your head you cannot tell what is going on. Handa sets out with seven different fruits and arrives with a basket of tangerines.
	The story is rich with mathematical ideas: the sequence or order of animals (monkey; ostrich; zebra; elephant; giraffe; antelope; parrot); the order fruit is taken (banana; guava; orange; mango; pineapple; avocado; passion fruit; and replaced with tangerines).
Simple detail (connecting story and real world)	There is the association between animal and fruit: banana/monkey; guava/ostrich; orange/zebra; mango/ elephant; pineapple/giraffe; avocado/antelope; passion fruit/parrot; and the goat disturbs the tangerines, which fill Handa's basket.
Fruit. Basket. Bringing a present to a friend. Planning a surprise.	**Number patterns and relations:** Subtraction of ones, from seven to zero: the mathematical idea of 'one less than' is silent but present, in the texture of the story. One less than seven is six; one less than six is five; one
Repetition (phrase)	less than five is four; one less than four is three; one less than three is two; one less than two is one; one less than one is none.
'will she like . . . or . . .?'	
Opening line	There is a harmonious relationship between the story idea and the mathematics. The mathematics is more of a consequence of the story. There is a pattern of number as seven is reduced to zero with each of the seven animals taking one fruit (subtraction). The pattern could be articulated by counting back in ones to zero.
'Handa put seven delicious fruits in a basket for her friend, Akeyo.'	

Mathematical possibilities: 'What if?'

Subtraction in ones from seven to zero: The story can be retold keeping the same plot and including phrases 'the monkey takes a banana, leaving six fruit in Handa's basket'.

Counting down: we change the starting number of fruit and count down in ones, twos, fives, tens or a combination of numbers. There could be 14 fruits with the seven animals taking two fruits each, counting down in twos 14, 12, 10, 8, 6, 4, 2, 0.

Doubles: if there are 14 fruits and each animal takes one, there will be seven fruit in the basket. The relationship between seven and 14 can be played with; seven is half of 14, 14 is double seven.

Appendix 4

Story profile: 'The Doorbell Rang' by Pat Hutchins

Structure and summary of story

Place Kitchen	**'The Doorbell Rang' by Pat Hutchins** Victoria and Sam are given a plate of 12 cookies to share, giving the possibility of six each. Two children arrive at the door so there are 12 cookies and four children, giving three each. Two more children arrive at the door, so there are six children, 12 cookies, and a possibility of two cookies each. Six more children arrive, so there are 12 children, 12 cookies, a possibility of one each. The doorbell rings again, presenting a dilemma. The mother suggests the children each eat the cookie they have on their plate before the door is answered, but Sam answers the door to Grandma, who is holding a large tray of cookies.
Characters Sam and Victoria	
Consciousness of character Children are aware of what is happening. At the end Sam looks through the letterbox and only he can see who is at the door.	**Illustrations:** These show increasing numbers of children arriving with muddy footprints. The pictures show the cookies divided, for example one cookie on each of 12 plates. One illustration shows Sam looking through the letter box to see who the last caller is.
Time (frame) Daytime; interval is unspecified	**Relationship between story and mathematics:** The illustrations show the mathematical idea of dividing using the principle of sharing, which connects closely to the story idea. The story idea is rich in mathematics. This is a case of the story expressing a mathematical idea harmoniously.
Plot (problem) The plate of 12 cookies needs to be shared between more and more people until it looks like there will be less than one cookie each. The last doorbell ring solves the problem as the caller has a large tray of cookies.	**Mathematical idea in the story:** Division based on equal sharing 'share equally between' (Haylock & Cockburn 2013). The number 12 is divided repeatedly by increasing numbers of children: 2, 4, 6 and 12 to give 6, 3, 2 and 1 cookies. There is the relationship between the 12 cookies being divided by an increasing number of children. 12 divided by 2 = 6 12 divided by 4 = 3 12 divided by 6 = 2 12 divided by 12 = 1 (this 12 is made up of six children already in the kitchen and two more children arrive with their four cousins 2 + 4 = 6)
Point of view Reader	

Events (sequence)	Mathematical language in the story: 'share them'; 'six each'; 'three each'; 'two each'; 'one each'; 'a lot'
Children are presented with a plate of 12 cookies. The doorbell rings four times. On the last ring the mother proposes that the cookies are eaten before the door opens. Sam looks through the letterbox. They wait and open to the last caller who has a large tray of cookies.	**Number patterns and number relationships:** The relationship between 12 divided by 4 = 3 and 12 divided by 3=4 could be exploited in an oral telling of the story. This pattern could be set out by changing the story of how the children arrive: there are two children and one arrives making three, then the doorbell rings and another arrives making four.
	A different pattern relating to division can be established by changing the number of biscuits: there could be 16 biscuits. The order of children is: two already there; two arrive; four arrive; eight arrive making a total of 16. The sequence could be 2, 4, 8, 16 children giving 8, 4, 2, 1 biscuits.
	16 divided by 2 = 8; 16 divided by 4 = 4; 16 divided by 8 = 2; 16 divided by 16 = 1.
Simple detail (connecting story and real world)	The story could be adapted to feature 20:
Kitchen Cookies Unexpected visitors	20 divided by 2 = 10; 20 divided by 4 = 5; 20 divided by 5 = 4; 20 divided by 10 = 2; 20 divided by 20 = 1.
	Connecting subtraction and division: the story can be played with in a way that brings subtraction and division together. The pattern can be changed by subtracting some cookies, which are eaten. There could be 20 cookies divided by two children giving ten each but then these two children eat two each leaving 20 – 4 = 16. The doorbell rings and two children arrive, so 16 cookies divided by four children = four cookies each. The four children then manage to eat two each, so 16 – 8 = 8 cookies left. Four more children arrive. Eight divided by eight leaves one each, which the children quickly eat.
Repetition (phrase)	
'No one makes cookies like Grandma', said Ma as the doorbell rang.	
Opening line	
'I've made some cookies for tea', said Ma.	
Mathematical possibilities: 'What if?'	
What if instead of 2, 4, 6 and 12 children the door opens to a pattern of 1, 3, 5 children (an odd number each time rather than even)?	
What if the original number of cookies were 15?	
What if the doorbell rings and children need to leave?	
What if we count how many cookies are on Grandma's tray, add these to the original 12 and share these between 12 children and two adults?	

Appendix 5

Story profile: 'Little Lumpty' by Miko Imai

	Structure and summary of story
	'Little Lumpty' by Miko Imai
Place Town of Dumpty where Humpty Dumpty had his fall	In the little town of Dumpty there was a high wall. Humpty Dumpty had fallen from it long, long ago. But people still remembered him.
Character Little Lumpty	Every day children played by the wall and sang, 'Humpty Dumpty sat on the wall. Humpty Dumpty had a great fall.' Little Lumpty loved the wall and always dreamed about climbing to the top.
Consciousness of character Lumpty is not immediately conscious of the fear of being at the top of the wall	'Don't ever do that', Lumpty's mother said. 'Remember, all the king's horses and all the king's men couldn't put Humpty Dumpty together again.' But Little Lumpty couldn't stop thinking about the wall. One day, on his way home from school, he found a long ladder and dragged it to the wall. He climbed up . . . and up . . . and up.
Time (frame) Late afternoon	At last he reached the top. 'Oh, there's my house! And there's my school! I can almost touch the clouds!' Lumpty was so happy that he danced along like a tightrope walker. 'If only my friends could see me now!' But then Little Lumpty looked down. IT WAS A BIG MISTAKE. His legs began to shake and tremble.
Plot (problem) Lumpty gets the idea into his head to climb the wall. He climbs up but cannot climb down. He needs to be rescued.	'Oh, no! I don't think I can get back to the ladder.' 'What if I'm not home by dinner time?' Darkness sets in and Little Lumpty remembers what happened to Humpty Dumpty. He screams for help. The people of the town spread out and hold a blanket, which he bounces on three times. He explains to his mother that he had to see what it was like on top of the wall. Little Lumpty tells the moon of his love of the wall, before falling asleep.
Point of view Little Lumpty's	

Events (sequence)

After school Lumpty finds a ladder. He climbs the wall. He is too frightened to come down. The people of the town get a blanket and he is rescued. Despite the fearful event he still loves the wall.

Simple detail (connecting story and real world)

Being warned by an adult not to do something. The ladder. Recognising detail of buildings (school). Tea and biscuits. The comfort of a bed and small toy.

Repetition (phrase)

Familiar phrase connecting to nursery rhyme:
'Humpty Dumpty sat on the wall. Humpty Dumpty had a great fall.'

Opening line

'In the little town of Dumpty there was a high wall.'

Mathematical possibilities: 'What if?'

Counting patterns (forwards and backwards)

Counting in ones: What if each rung on the ladder equals the height of a brick? On retelling the story Lumpty could count as he goes up each step of the ladder 1, 2, 3, 4, 5, 6, 7, 8, 9, 10, 11, 12.

Counting in multiples of a number:

What if the gap between the rungs of the ladder equates with two bricks? As Lumpty goes up the ladder he counts 2, 4, 6, 8, 10, 12, 14, 16, 18, 20, 22, 24.

What if the gap between the rungs of the ladder equates with five bricks? As Lumpty goes up the ladder he counts 5, 10, 15, 20, 25, 30, 35, 40, 45, 50, 55, 60.

Multiplication:

What if a row of bricks or course is made of five bricks: one lot of five is five, two lots of five is ten, three lots of five is 15, four lots of five is 20, five lots of five is 25, six lots of five is 30, seven lots of five is 35, eight lots of five is 40, nine lots of five is 45, ten lots of five is 50, 11 lots of five is 55, 12 lots of five is 60.

Illustrations: The idea of the high wall is presented. Lumpty's love of the wall is communicated with the image of him washing off chalk graffiti. The height perspective from the top is illustrated in a way that conveys fear. The comfort of the return home is seen in the final picture where Lumpty is asleep in bed.

Relationship between story and mathematics: The story is simple. It's about climbing a wall despite having been warned not to. The reason for the warning is realised when Lumpty is too frightened to climb back down. The story is rich with mathematical ideas.

The following mathematical themes fall out of the story: height of wall; historical time 'long, long, ago'; history (historical fall of Humpty); time changing over a day (dinner time and getting dark); length of long ladder; up; top; perspective from a distance (looking down from a height); down; distance across top of wall to ladder; size of blanket (big); stretched (area and tautness); bottom of wall; number of people to hold the blanket (4 sides x 3 people = 12 in total); bounced 'once, twice, three times'.

Mathematical language in the story: 'long' ; 'up'; 'top'; 'down'; 'bottom'; 'once'; 'twice' ; 'three times.'

Number patterns and relations: There is a harmonious relationship between story and mathematical ideas. There is a pattern of number as Lumpty bounces 'once, twice, three times . . . and then came safely to rest on the blanket'. There are opportunities to draw out mathematical possibilities and preserve the plot of this story.

Counting in multiples of a number: We can describe a relationship between the gap between the rungs of the ladder and the equivalent number of the bricks of the wall. This relationship can be used to count in multiples of a number and to calculate how many bricks high the wall is.

What if each rung of the ladder is equivalent to two bricks of the wall? There is an opportunity here for counting in multiples of two as each rung of the ladder will bring Little Lumpty up two bricks and the count could be: 2, 4, 6, 8, 10, 12, 14, 16, 18, 20, 22, 24 if a ladder with 12 rungs brings Little Lumpty to the top of the wall. Or there could be an opportunity for counting in multiples of five as each rung of the ladder could bring Little Lumpty up five bricks: 5,10,15, 20, 25, 30, 35, 40, 45, 50, 55, 60.

Appendix 6

How to make a gorilla hand puppet

How to make a gorilla hand puppet

You will need –

- Template for hand puppet
- Black felt – 25 cm x 30 cm (x2)
- Grey felt – 15 cm x 15 cm
- 2 buttons
- Cotton wool (for stuffing)

Equipment –

- Needle
- Thread (black and grey)
- Sewing machine
- Scissors
- Pins

1. Trace the hand puppet template onto the black felt and cut out two.

2. Cut out a shape for the gorilla's face from the grey felt.

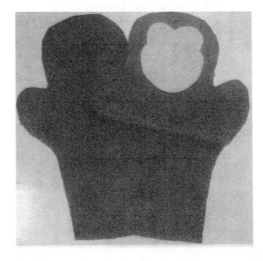

Appendix 6: how to make a gorilla hand puppet . . . *continued*

3. Sew on the face with a needle and grey thread and leave a small gap for the stuffing.

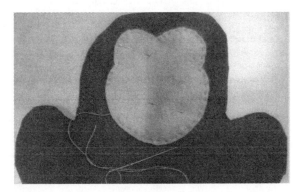

4. Stuff the lower half of the face with cotton woll, stitch up the gap and embellish the face with facial features (two button eyes, nose and mouth).

Appendix 6: how to make a gorilla hand puppet . . . *continued*

5. Sew the two main pieces of puppet together using a sewing machine and black thread with the face on the inside.

6. Stitch all the way around the puppet and turn it inside out so that its face is on the outside.

7. Put your hand inside the puppet to straighten it out and it is ready to use!

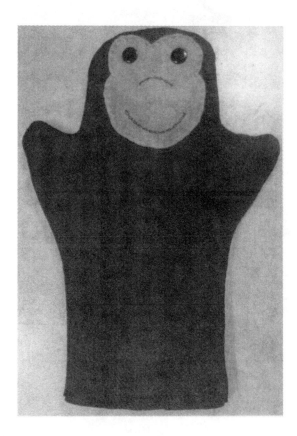

References

Adcock, R. (2013a) 'Oral Mathematical Story Project: Good Night Gorilla retold by Rachel Adcock'. Audio and video recorded by Caroline McGrath for unpublished thesis, Plymouth University, 14 June.

Adcock, R. (2013b) 'Oral Mathematical Story Project: Discussion about experience creating and using props and puppets'. Interview with Caroline McGrath for unpublished thesis, Plymouth University, 14 June.

Allison, C. (1987) *I'll Tell You a Story, I'll Sing You a Song: A parents' guide to the fairy tales, fables, songs, and rhymes of childhood*. New York: Dell Publishing.

Arnold, K. (1994) *Knock, Knock, Teremok!* New York: North-South Books.

Baxter, J. (2005) 'Some Reflections on Problem Posing: A conversation with Marion Walter', *Teaching Children Mathematics*, 12 (3), October, pp.122–128.

Beck, I. (2004) *The Enormous Turnip*. Oxford: Oxford University Press.

Belsten, R. (2013a) 'Oral Mathematical Story Project: The Shoemaker and the Elves retold by Rebecca Belsten'. Audio and video recorded by Caroline McGrath for unpublished thesis, Plymouth University, 14 June.

Belsten, R. (2013b) 'Oral Mathematical Story Project: Discussion about experience creating and using props and puppets'. Interview with Caroline McGrath for unpublished thesis, Plymouth University, 14 June.

Blake, W. (1905) 'The Tyger', in J. Sampson (ed.) *The Poetical Works of William Blake: A new and verbatim text from the manuscript engraved and letterpress originals*. Oxford: Clarendon Press, pp. 110–111.

Booker, C. (2004) *The Seven Basic Plots: Why we tell stories*. London: Continuum.

Brown, P. (2013a) *Teremok* [oral storytelling to Ashley Down Infants School]. 25 January.

Brown, P. (2013b) Stone Soup [oral storytelling to Ashley Down Infants School]. 25 January.

Brown, P. (2013c) 'Oral Mathematical Storytelling from a Storytellers Perspective'. Interviewed by Caroline McGrath for unpublished PhD thesis. Plymouth University, 13 May.

Brown, P. (2013d) 'Bristol Storytelling Festival'. Bristol, 1 February.

Brown, T. (2003) *Meeting the Standards in Primary Mathematics: A guide to the ITT NC*. London: Routledge Falmer.

Browne, E. (1998) *Handa's Surprise*. London: Walker Books.

Browne, E. (2013) E-mail to Caroline McGrath, 26 July.

Browne, E. and Parkins, D. (1993) *No Problem!* London: Walker Books.

Bruner, J. (1986) *Actual Minds, Possible Worlds*. Cambridge: Harvard University Press.

Bryant, S. C. (1947) *How to Tell Stories to Children: And some stories to tell*. London: George G. Harrap and co. Ltd.

Burns, K. (2013a) 'Oral Mathematical Story Project: Discussion about experience including oral story as part of an interview for employment'. Interview with Caroline McGrath for unpublished thesis, 23 July.

Burns, K. (2013b) 'Oral Mathematical Story Project: The Enormous Turnip retelling with a small group'. Audio and video recorded by Caroline McGrath for unpublished thesis, 23 July.

Burns, M. (1994) *The Greedy Triangle*. London: Scholastic.

Burroway, J. (2009) E-mail to Caroline McGrath, July.

Carr, M. (2001) *Assessment in Early Childhood Settings: Learning stories*. London: SAGE Publications Ltd.

Casey, R. (1999) 'A key concepts model for teaching and learning mathematics', *Mathematics in School, 28*(3): 29–31.

Casey, R. (2011) 'Teaching mathematically promising children', in V. Koshy, and J. Murray (eds) *Unlocking Mathematics Teaching* (2nd edition). Oxon: Routledge, pp.124–150.

Cheshire, L. (2013) 'Oral Mathematical Story Project: Experience as part of the research project'. Interview with Caroline McGrath for unpublished thesis, 21 June.

Churchill, W. (2005) *Never Give In!: Winston Churchill's greatest speeches* [CD]. BBC Audiobooks Ltd.

Coles, A. (2013a) *Being Alongside: For the teaching and learning of mathematics*. Seminar Graduate School of Education, Bristol University. 6 June

Coles, A. (2013b) 'On Metacognition', *For the Learning of Mathematics*, 33 (1): 21–26.

Corbett, P. (2006) *The Bumper Book of Storytelling into Writing Key Stage 1*. Wiltshire: Clown Publishing.

Corbett, P. (2007) 'Developing Creative Writing Skills'. Available at http://www.learning-works.org.uk/index.php?id=566 (accessed 19 February 2014).

Craft, A. (2001) *Creativity and Early Years Education: A lifewide foundation*. London: Continuum.

Davies, A. (2007) *Storytelling in the Classroom: Enhancing traditional oral skills for teachers and pupils*. London: Paul Chapman Publishing.

Dodd, L. and Sutton, E. (1978) *My Cat Likes to Hide in Boxes*. London: Penguin.

Egan, K. (1988) *Teaching as Storytelling: An alternative approach to teaching and the curriculum*. London: Routledge.

Fairclough, R. (2011) 'Developing Problem-Solving Skills in Mathematics', in V. Koshy and J. Murray (eds), *Unlocking Mathematics Teaching* (2nd edn). Oxon: Routledge, pp. 84–109.

Fisher, R. (2009) *Creative Dialogue: Talk for thinking in the classroom*. Oxon: Routledge.

Forest, H. (1998) *Stone Soup*. Arkanas: August House LittleFolk.

Frobisher, L. (1999) 'Primary School Children's Knowledge of Odd and Even Numbers', in O. Orton (ed), *Pattern in the Teaching and Learning of Mathematics*. London: Cassell, pp. 31–48.

Frobisher, L., Monaghan, J., Orton, A., Orton, J., Roper, T. and Threlfall, J. (1999) *Learning to Teach Number: A handbook for students and teachers in the primary school*. Cheltenham: Nelson Thornes.

Gallas, K. (1995) *Talking Their Way Into Science: Hearing children's questions and theories, responding with curricula*. New York: Teachers College Press.

Ginnis, S. and Ginnis, P. (2006) *Covering the Curriculum with Stories: Six cross-curricular projects that teach literacy and thinking through dramatic play*. Wales: Crown House Publishing Ltd.

Grimm Brothers (1995) *The Elves and the Shoemaker*. Stafford: Nutshell Publishing Ltd.

Grugeon, E. and Gardner, P. (2000) *The Art of Storytelling for Teachers and Pupils: Using stories to develop literacy in primary classrooms*. London: David Fulton.

Hartman, B. (2002) *Anyone Can Tell a Story: Bob Hartman's guide to storytelling*. Oxon: Lion Hudson plc.

Haylock, D. (2006) *Mathematics Explained for Primary Teachers* (3rd edn). London: SAGE.

Haylock, D. and Cockburn, A. (2013) *Understanding Mathematics for Young Children* (4th edn). London: SAGE.

Haynes, J. and Murris, K. (2012) *Picturebooks, Pedagogy and Philosophy*. Oxon: Routledge.

Hersh, R. (1998) *What Is Mathematics Really?* London: Vintage.

Hong, H. (1996) 'Effects of Mathematics Learning Through Children's Literature on Math Achievement and Dispositional Outcomes', *Early Childhood Research Quarterly*, (11): 477–494.

Hughes, M. (1986) *Children and Number: Difficulties in learning mathematics*. Oxford: Blackwell Publishers Ltd.

Hutchins, P. (1986) *The Doorbell Rang*. New York, Greenwillow Books.

Imai, M. (1994) *Little Lumpty*. London: Walker Books.

Keat, J. B. and Wilburne, J. M. (2009) 'The Impact of Storybooks on Kindergarten Children's Mathematical Achievement and Approaches to Learning', *US-China Education Review*,6 (7) serial no.56 p61–67. Available at http://www.eric.ed.gov/ERICWebPortal/search/detailmini. jsp?_nfpb=true&_&ERICExtSearch_SearchValue_0=ED506319&ERICExtSearch_SearchType_ 0=no&accno=ED506319 (accessed 6 October 2011).

Kelham, S. (2013a) 'Oral Mathematical Story Project: "My Cat Likes to Hide in Boxes"'. Interview with Caroline McGrath for unpublished thesis, 22 February.

Kelham, S. (2013b) 'Oral Mathematical Story Project: Experience as part of the research project'. Interview with Caroline McGrath for unpublished thesis, 21 June.

Kelham, S. (2013c) 'Oral Mathematical Story Project: "Blue Egg Dinosaur" story telling small group'. Audio and video recorded by Caroline McGrath for unpublished thesis, 21 March.

Kelham, S. (2013d) 'Oral Mathematical Story Project: "Penguin" story telling with small group'. Audio and video recorded by Caroline McGrath for unpublished thesis, 5 July.

Koshy, V. (2001) *Teaching Mathematics to Able Children*. London: David Fulton.

Kuyvenhoven, J. (2009) *In the Presence of Each Other: A pedagogy of storytelling*. London: University of Toronto Press Incorporated.

Lave, J. and Wenger, E. (1991) *Situated Learning: Legitimate peripheral participation*. Cambridge: Cambridge University Press.

Lewis, K. (1992) *Floss*. London: Walker Books.

Lipke, B. (1996) *Figures, Facts and Fables: Telling tales in science and maths*. Portsmouth NH: Heinemann.

Lipman, D. (1999) *Improving Your Storytelling: Beyond the basics for all who tell stories in work or play*. Arkansas: August House Publishers, INC.

Lord, J. V. and Burroway, J. (1972) *The Giant Jam Sandwich*. Basingstoke: Macmillan Children's Books.

Mason, J. (1989) 'Mathematical Abstraction as a Result of a Delicate Shift of Attention', *For the Learning of Mathematics*, 9 (2): 2–8.

Matterson, E. (1991) *This Little Puffin*. London: Penguin Group.

McGrath, C. (2010) *Supporting Early Mathematical Development: Practical approaches to play-based learning*. Oxon: Routledge.

McGrath, C. (2012a) 'From Posing to Solving', *Early Years Educator,* 14 (4).

McGrath, C. (2012b) 'Problem Posing: Problem solving'. Presentation for Torbay Local Education Authority at Torbay Early Years Maths Conference, Torbay. 12th June.

McGrath, C. (2013) Private notes. Unpublished PhD research thesis. Plymouth University.

McGrath, C. (2014) 'Mathematical Storyteller Kings and Queens: An alternative pedagogical choice to facilitate mathematical thinking and understand children's mathematical capabilities', in S. Chinn (Ed.), *The International Handbook for Mathematical Difficulties and Dyscalculia*. Oxon: Routledge.

McQuillan, M. (ed.) (2000) *The Narrative Reader*. London: Routledge.

Mercer, N. (2000) *Words and Minds: How we use language to think together*. London: Routledge.

Merttens, R. (1987) *Teaching Primary Mathematics*. London: Edward Arnold.

Naik, M. (2013) 'Mathematics', in R. Jones and D. Wyse (eds), *Creativity in the Primary Curriculum* (2nd edn). Oxon: Routledge, pp. 33–49.

Oxford Dictionary (2012) *Paperback Oxford English Dictionary* (7th edn). Oxford: Oxford University Press.

Paley, V. G. (1981) *Wally's Stories: Conversations in the kindergarten*. London: Harvard University Press.

Paley, V. G. (1999) *The Kindness of Children*. London: Harvard University Press.

Parkinson, R. (2011) *Storytelling and Imagination: Beyond basic literacy 8–14*. Oxon: Routledge.

Play for Tomorrow (1991) BBC Television (date of transmission unknown).

Polya, G. (1945) *How to Solve It: A new aspect of mathematical method* (2nd edn). Princeton, NJ: Princeton University Press.

Pound, L. (2006) *Supporting Mathematical Development in the Early Years* (2nd edn). Berkshire: Open University Press.

Pound, L. (2008) *Thinking and Learning about Mathematics in the Early Years*. Oxon: Routledge.

Pound, L. and Lee, T. (2011) *Teaching Mathematics Creatively*. Oxon: Routledge.

Pratt, N. (2006) *Interactive Maths Teaching in the Primary School*. London: Paul Chapman.

Ransome, A. (2003) *Old Peter's Russian Tales*. London: Jane Nissen Books.

Rathmann, P. (2012) *Good Night Gorilla*. London: Egmont.

Rayner, C. (2008) *Augustus and His Smile*. London: Mantra Lingua.

Rogoff, B. (2003) *The Cultural Nature of Human Development*. Oxford: Oxford University Press.

Schiro, M. (2004) *Oral Storytelling and Teaching Mathematics: Pedagogical and multicultural perspectives*. California: SAGE.

Shakespeare, W. (2009) 'The Tempest' in Knowles, E. *Oxford Dictionary of Quotations* (7th edn). Oxford: Oxford University Press, pp. 733–734.

Smith, C. (2007) *One City, Two Brothers*. Bath: Barefoot Books.

Stanford, P. (2012) 'Stop Telling Children Maths Isn't for Them', *Telegraph Weekend* (Saturday), 20 October, p.13.

Suggate, J., Davis, A. and Goulding, M. (2006) *Mathematical Knowledge for Primary Teachers* (3rd edn). Oxon: Routledge.

Suggate, J., Davis. A. and Goulding, M. (2010) *Mathematical Knowledge for Primary Teachers* (4th edn). Oxon: Routledge.

Talk for Writing (2008) Presented by P. Corbett [DVD]. Nottingham: DCSF Publications.

The Book of LIEH-TZU: A Classic of the Tao (1990) Translated by A. C. Graham. London: HarperCollins, pp. 99–101.

Toy Hong, L. (1993) *Two of Everything*. Chicago, IL: Albert Whitman and Company.

Van den Heuvel-Panhuizen, M. and Elia, I. (2012) 'Developing a Framework for the Evaluation of Picturebooks That Support Kindergartners' Learning of Mathematics', *Research in Mathematics Education,* 14 (1): 17–47. University of Plymouth. Available at http://dx.doi.org/ 10.1080/14794802.2012.657437 (accessed 19 February 2014).

Van den Heuvel-Panhuizen, M. and Van den Boogaard, S. (2008) 'Picture Books as an Impetus for Kindergartners' Mathematical Thinking', *Mathematical Thinking and Learning,* 10 (4): 341–373. University of Plymouth. Available at http://dx.doi.org/10.1080/10986060802425539 (accessed 19 February 2014).

Vygotsky, L. (1978) *Mind in Society: The development of higher psychological processes.* Translated by M. Cole, V. John-Steiner, S. Scribner and E. Souberman (eds), London: The MTI Press.

Walker, B. (1975) *We Made a Story.* London: J. Garnet Miller Ltd.

Walshe, L. (2013) 'Oral Mathematical Story Project: Discussion after Little Lumpty'. Interview with Caroline McGrath for unpublished thesis, 23 November.

Weaver, S. (2013) 'Number Stories' [Lecture to Foundation Degree Early Childhood Studies year one]. 21 November.

Welchman-Tischler, R. (1992) *How to Use Children's Literature to Teach Mathematics.* USA: The National Council of Teachers of Mathematics.

Wye, C. (2013a) 'Oral Mathematical Story Project'. Telephone interview with Caroline McGrath for unpublished thesis, Plymouth University, 24 July.

Wye, C (2013b) 'Training Oral Story: Augustus retold by Cassandra Wye' [Lecture to Foundation Degree Early Childhood Studies year one]. 30 January.

Wye, C. (2013c) 'Oral Mathematical Story Project: The Man Who Moved a Mountain' [Lecture to Foundation Degree Early Childhood Studies year one]. 29 January.

Yeats, W. B. (1912) *Poems.* London: T. Fisher Unwin Ltd.

Yeats, W. B. (1928) *The Tower.* London: Macmillan and Co. Ltd.

Bibliography

Boaler, J. (2009) *The Elephant in the Classroom: Helping children learn and love maths*. London: Souvenir Press Ltd.

Boden, M. A. (2001) 'Creativity and Knowledge', in A. Craft, B. Jeffrey and M. Leibling (eds), *Creativity in Education*. London: Continuum, pp.95–102.

Brizuela, B. (2004) *Mathematical Development in Young Children Exploring Notations*. New York: Teachers College Press.

Bruce, T. (2001) *Learning through Play: Babies, toddlers and the foundation years*. London: Hodder Arnold.

Bruce, T. (2011) *Cultivating Creativity for Babies, Toddlers and Young Children*. London: Hodder Education.

Carlsen, M. (2013) 'Engaging with mathematics in the kindergarten. Orchestrating a fairy tale through questioning and use of tools', *European Early Childhood Education Research Journal*, 21(4), 502–513.

Clemson, D. and Clemson, W. (1994) *Mathematics in the Early Years*. London: Routledge.

Egan, K. (1989) *Memory, Imagination and Learning: Connected by the story*. Available at http://www.educ.sfu.ca/kegan/Memorylm.html (accessed 31 March 2014).

Eun, B. (2010) 'From Learning to Development: A sociocultural approach to instruction', *Cambridge Journal of Education,* 40 (4): December 2010, pp. 401–418.

Fox, C. (1995) 'Storytelling at Home and at School', in R. Campbell and L. Miller (eds), *Supporting Children in the Early Years*. Staffordshire: Trentham Books Ltd.

Fox, C. (2003) 'Playing the Storyteller: Some principles for learning literacy in the early years of schooling', in N. Hall, J. Larson and J. Marsh (eds), *Handbook of Early Childhood Literacy*. London: SAGE, pp.189–196.

Gamble, N. and Yates, S. (2008) *Exploring Children's Literature* (2nd edn). London: SAGE Publications Ltd.

Garvey, C. (1984) *Children's Talk*. Oxford: Fontana Paperbacks. (The Developing Child).

Griffiths, N. (2007) *Stories Can be Counted on! Ideas for developing mathematics through story*. Wiltshire: Corner to Learn.

Haringham (2001) 'Effective Teaching and Learning: The role of the creative parent–teacher', in A. Craft, B. Jeffrey and M. Leibling (eds), *Creativity in Education*. London: Continuum, pp.152–157.

Haylock, D., and Thangata, F. (2007) *Key Concepts in Teaching Primary Mathematics*. London: SAGE Publications.

Hobart, C. and Frankel, J. (2004) *A Practical Guide to Child Observation and Assessment* (3rd edn). Cheltenham: Nelson Thornes.

Holt, M., and Dienes, Z. (1973) *Let's Play Maths*. Middlesex: Penguin Books.

Hughes, M. (1996) *Progression in Learning (BERA Dialogues)* (ed). Clevedon: Multilingual Matters.

Hughes, M. Desforges, C. and Mitchell C. (2000) *Numeracy and Beyond: Applying mathematics in the primary school*. Buckingham: Open University Press.

Jack, A. (2010) *Pop Goes the Weasel: The secret meanings of nursery rhymes*. London: Penguin.

Joubert, M. (2001) 'The Art of Creative Teaching: NACCCE and beyond', in A. Craft, B. Jeffrey and M. Leibling (eds), *Creativity in Education*. London: Continuum, pp.17–34.

Kline, M. (1987) *Mathematics in Western Culture: A fascinating assessment of a science that has contributed immeasurably to our civilization*. London: Penguin Books.

Koshy, V. and Murray, J. (2011) *Unlocking Mathematics Teaching* (2nd edn). Oxon: Routledge.

Kozulin, A. (1990) *Vygotsky's Psychology: A biography of ideas*. Hertfordshire: Harvester Wheatsheaf.

Leeper, M. (2011) 'Life in Another Language', *Early Years Educator,* 12 (12): April, pp.v–vii.

MakeBelieve Arts (2002) *Our Philosophy: The unique power of story*. Available at http://www.makebelievearts.co.uk/Information/About+Us/Our+Philosophy (accessed 31 March 2014).

Merttens, R., (2009) Ruth Merttens Describes the New Maths Teaching Sequence. Available at http://www.hamilton-trust.org.uk/standard.asp?id=8995 (accessed 19 February 2014).

National Advisory Committee on Creative and Cultural Education (1999) *All Our Futures: Creativity, culture and education*. Suffolk: DfEE Publications.

Ong, J. (2002) *Orality and Literacy: The technologizing of the word*. London: Routledge.

Palmer, S. and Corbett, P. (2003) *Literacy: What Works? The golden rules of primary literacy and how you can use them in your classroom*. Cheltenham: Nelson Thornes.

Pimm, D. (1987) *Speaking Mathematically: Communication in mathematics classrooms*. London: Routledge and Kegan Paul.

Pratt, N. (2011) 'Mathematics outside the classroom', in S. Waite (Ed.), *Children Learning Outside the Classroom: Birth to Eleven*. London: SAGE Publications, pp.80–93.

Razfar, A. and Gutierrez, K. (2003) 'Reconceptualising Early Childhood Literacy: The sociocultural influence', in N. Hall, J. Larson and J. Marsh (eds) *Handbook of Early Childhood Literacy*. London: SAGE, pp. 34–49.

Roemer, M. (1995) *Telling Stories: Postmodernism and the invalidation of traditional narrative*. London: Rowman and Littlefield Publishers

Rowland, T., Turner, F., Thwaites, A. and Huckstep, P. (2009) *Developing Primary Mathematics Teaching*. London: SAGE.

Schoenfeld, A. (1996) 'In Fostering Communities of Inquiry, Must It Matter That the Teacher Knows "the Answer"?', *For the Learning of Mathematics,* 16 (3), 11–16.

Sfard, A. and Kieran, C. (2001) 'Cognition as Communication: Rethinking Learning-by-Talking through Multi-Faceted Analysis of Students' Mathematical Interactions', *Mind, Culture, and Activity*, 8 (1), 42–76.

Smidt, S. (2009) *Introducing Vygotsky: A guide for practitioners and students in early years education*. Oxon: Routledge.

Stevenson, P. (2013) *Tales from Smugglers Cove* [storytelling to public]. 31 July.

Treffers, A., and Beishuizen, M. (1999) 'Realistic Mathematics Education in the Netherlands', in I. Thompson (Ed.) *Issues in Teaching Numeracy in Primary Schools*. Buckingham: Open University Press, pp.27–38.

University of Cambridge (2014) *Dramatic Mathematics: nrich.maths.org*. Available at http://nrich.maths.org/2433/index (accessed 31 March 2014).

Vygotsky, L. (1934) *Thought and Language*. Translated by A. Kozulin (Ed.). London: The MTI Press.

Wertsch, J. V. (1991) *Voices of the Mind: A sociocultural approach to mediated action*. Cambridge, MA: Harvard University Press.

Wye, C. (2005) *The Story Pot Storytelling with Early Years*. Available at http://www.storiesin motion.co.uk/The_Story_Pot_storytelling_with_Early_Years.pdf (accessed 31 March 2014).

Zipes, J. (2006) *Why Fairy Tales Stick: The evolution and relevance of a genre*. Oxon: Routledge.

Childrens' books referenced

Arnold, K. (1994) *Knock, Knock, Teremok!* New York: North-South Books.

Beck, I. (2004) *The Enormous Turnip*. Oxford: Oxford University Press.

Browne, E. (1998) *Handa's Surprise*. London: Walker Books.

Browne, E. and Parkins, D. (1993) *No Problem!* London: Walker Books.

Burns, M. (1994) *The Greedy Triangle*. London: Scholastic.

Dodd, L. and Sutton, E. (1978) *My Cat Likes to Hide in Boxes*. London: Penguin.

Forest, H. (1998) *Stone Soup*. Arkanas: August House LittleFolk.

Grimm Brothers (1995) *The Elves and the Shoemaker*. Stafford: Nutshell Publishing Ltd.

Hutchins, P. (1986) *The Doorbell Rang*. New York, Greenwillow Books.

Imai, M. (1994) *Little Lumpty*. London: Walker Books.

Lewis, K. (1992) *Floss*. London: Walker Books.

Lord, J. V. and Burroway, J. (1972) *The Giant Jam Sandwich*. Basingstoke: Macmillan Children's Books.

Matterson, E. (1991) *This Little Puffin*. London: Penguin Group.

Ransome, A. (2003) *Old Peter's Russian Tales*. London: Jane Nissen Books.

Rathmann, P. (2012) *Good Night Gorilla*. London: Egmont.

Rayner, C. (2008) *Augustus and His Smile*. London: Mantra Lingua.

Smith, C. (2007) *One City, Two Brothers*. Bath: Barefoot Books.

Toy Hong, L. (1993) *Two of Everything*. Chicago, IL: Albert Whitman and Company.

Index

'A Faery Song' 83

a freer and more relaxed storyteller 86

ability: children categorised as lower 66, 94, 140; to create story 4; to imagine 23; of lower 67, 69; and observation of Jake 43; of the storyteller 79; to think mathematically 142

abstract: concepts 31; and concrete 141; concrete to 30, 100; to concrete 36, 100, 108, 111; experience 118; fantasy stories 30; features of story 111; generalising and 71; idea 1, 41, 105, 111; ideas 31–2, 34–5, 44, 141; learning 30–2; mathematics 31, 32; the mathematical concept 81; mathematical ideas 32, 34, 106, 111, 128, 140; mathematical ideas and concrete story props 120; mathematical and story ideas 99, 100, 140; nature of oral story 99, 100, 105; question 100; story ideas 140; suggestion 110; or symbolic learning 30; terms 31; thought 35, 44; see also concrete; see also props and puppets

abstraction: mathematical 80, 81,99, 111; from words 98, 141

accessible: commutative principle of addition makes calculations 91; ideas about teaching maths 133, 142; making difficult subjects 1

achievement 47, 48, 99

Adcock, R. 105

addition: algorithm 12, 17, 42; commutative principle of 91, 93; complements 121; concept of 90; developing an understanding about 91; and division 50, 53, 55–6; grasp of 14; ideas 91; language of 90; as a learning supportive characteristic 55; mathematical maps for 132; mathematical story of 52; multiplication as repeated 61, 64; patterns

14; playing with 124; sequential 104; story 52–3; story based on 90; and subtraction 41, 124, 132; structures 90–1, 93; as the union of two sets 90

Aeroplane 6

algebraic representation 14

algorithm 12, 17, 42, 144

Allison, C. 95, 128, 130

alongside: 87; and 'Blue Egg Dinosaur' story 93; children 4, 143; oral story as an approach 140; in play 35; in smaller groups 4, 87–9, 96, 143

Among School Children 97

Arnold, K. 33, 34, 119, 128

assessment of learning 7; see also mathematical observation

audio recording: free Routledge download 4; for mathematical observation 7, 16, 41, 42, 43; retelling stories 65 and; of stories informing research 70, 77, 83, 90, 97, 103, 112, 117, 123, 128

Augustus 1, 105, 111, 143

autistic 66, 68, 140

Baxter, J. 11

behaviour: and classroom expectations 76; as a factor around telling stories 75; for learning 86; as a storyteller 86; see also mathematical behaviour; see also small groups

Belsten, R. 98, 99, 102, 105

Blake, William 1, 2

'Blue Egg Dinosaur' story 90, 91, 93

Booker, C. 23, 28

Brown, P. 33, 34, 37, 46, 64, 73, 77, 105, 121, 127, 128

Brown, T. 11

Browne, E. 1, 21–22, 47, 95, 100, 120, 132, 148

Browne, E. and Parkins, D. 6–8, 16, 27
Bruner, J. 25, 27, 28
Bryant, S. C. 25, 26, 27, 65, 95, 128, 130
Burns, K. 81, 127–28, 129
Burns, M. 47, 83–84, 86, 88, 123–24, 128
Burroway, J. 1, 47

camper van 37
capacity: for creativity 12; for explicit teaching
    142; and the story 'Teremok' 38, 121, 128
cardinal number 90
careful crafting of story and mathematics
    134–135
Carr, M. 2, 7, 12, 15, 17, 41, 141
Casey, R. 7, 12, 13, 14, 15, 66, 141
catalytic 48; see also motivation
challenge: of capturing children's mathematical
    behaviour 16; creative 128; of framing
    mathematics 12; in learning 81; 'Little
    Lumpty' 59, 61; mathematical maps 132: for
    the mathematical storyteller 134; of oral
    mathematical storytelling 136; problem
    presents a 11; of retelling a story 113, 129; to
    storytellers 32, 56; of working with story 29
challenges: children set themselves 113; of
    creative mathematical teaching 2, 74; the
    need to move from concrete to abstract 30;
    of oral mathematical story 3–4, 71, 74,
    125–7, 134; oral storytelling 112–3;
    positioning mathematical ideas 81; and
    surprises 82; teacher assumptions 67, 69;
    'The Greedy Triangle' story 88; thinking 10,
    43, 125
checking: and conjecture 12; and mathematical
    process 15; for reasonableness 11; when
    counting 16; see also strategy
Cheshire, L. 84, 85, 88, 134
children playing with story: as storytellers 112,
    120, 121–125, 139–140; 'Ladybird on a Leaf'
    38, 39, 40, 44, 50; 'Little Lumpty' 57, 62,
    122; 'Penguin' 122, 143; 'Teremok' 34, 38,
    44, 121; 'The Greedy Triangle' 124
Churchill, W. 126
classifying and sorting 15
clipboard 77, 78
cognitive 29, 46; and cognitively 54, 55
Coles, A. 87
collective: about the class collectively 66;
    collective thinking nourishes individuals 72,
    73; observing collectively 76, 77
complements of a number 91

concentration 27, 66
concrete: to abstract 30, 31, 100; and play 36;
    representation of ideas with puppets and
    props 99, 100, 106, 108, 111, 120, 141; see
    also abstract; see also props and puppets
confidence: and repetition 27; as a storyteller
    99, 105–6, 110, 111, 120, 127, 140; in
    manipulating numbers 18, 62; teaching
    maths i; quieter children 93; and scaffold
    105–106; and employability 127; see also
    props and puppets
conjecture: definition of 12, 13; and
    mathematical observation tool 17, 42; as
    conjectural question 35, 41, 140
connections: between addition and division 56;
    building up 7, 113; between ideas and
    concepts 73; make mathematical 4, 7, 13,
    93, 96, 134, 136; making a map of 142;
    making mathematical 2, 10, 15, 17, 42, 88–9,
    144; mathematical 64, 70–1, 77, 113;
    between mathematical ideas 53, 71, 82;
    network of 65, 90; in observations 41–2;
    between story and memory 72; repetitive
    phrases as 130; to previous examples 115;
    and seeing patterns 132; within stories 121;
    between story and mathematics 21, 60, 69,
    120, 137; see also creative dialogue
connections: mathematical 2, 4, 7; with stories
    121
Corbett, P. 65, 130
counting: abstraction 80; accurately 118,
    121; and adding 118, 121; adding and
    subtracting 120; back 149; considered
    3; checking 16; down 149; errors 16;
    mathematical processes 15; in multiples
    30, 57, 59–69, 77, 123, 131, 142, 153;
    on 91, 93; in ones 61, 102, 123, 125, 153;
    opportunity 69; pattern 62, 84, 153; repeated
    80; strategies 104; in threes 123; in twos
    62–68, 102, 106; in zoomy numbers 123;
    see also addition
Craft, A. 13, 35
creative: capacity for 12; use of 32; classroom
    experience 67; creating problems 11;
    pedagogical approach 69; in play 36, 37;
    problem in story 50; see also creative
    dialogue
creative dialogue: allows fresh connections 89;
    encouraging children to engage in 82;
    features of 71; following 'The Greedy Triangle'
    88; multiple directions 75; oral mathematical

story and 82; as part of smaller group experiences 84; playful quality of 73–4; prompting possibility thinking through 89; prompting possibility through 83

creative mathematical dialogue: experiences evoke 96; extracts of children's 73–4, 88, 92–3, 102, 124; facilitating 32, 82, 143; gauging children's participation 32; oral mathematical story and 82; as part of flexible story 143; puppets and props spark 99

creative mathematical thinking: facilitating children's 4; making puppets and props 106, 108, 110, 111; oral story and mathematical ideas support 124

cultural development 71

culture: a child's understanding of 28; of genuine participation 76; mathematics as part of human 1; oral story and mathematics positively disrupt 69; school 67; classroom 69; and stories 28–9

curiosity 11, 12, 17, 24, 42, 47, 144

curricula 30, 51

curriculum 1, 28, 109

denominator 52, 53, 55

design detail: 'Little Lumpty' 106, 107

dialogue: creative mathematical 32; encouragingchildren to engage in creative 82; mathematical 84, 114

discourse 20, 22, 23, 24, 25, 32, 56

disposition 12, 13, 16, 36, 48, 50, 51, 56

distance 29, 37, 60, 153

division: and algorithm 12; and pattern 14; in context of a story 50, 52–3, 55, 56, 150, 151

Dodd, L. and Sutton, E. 48

doubling 15, 74, 134

educational implications 51

Egan, K. 30, 31, 100, 141

emotion: and cognitive 46; and development 48, 55; and disposition 12; engages emotionally 54, 55; and relationships 61

employability 127

engage: in creative dialogue 82; in mathematical thinking 2, 32, 49, 139, 143; small groups 93, 94; with the story 74, 77, 81, 127

engagement: autistic child 68; children 76–7; deeper 89, 96; emotional and cognitive 46, 55; feature of creative dialogue 71; and meaningful mathematics 47

English as a Second Language 43, 66, 68, 95–6, 140

environment 4, 48, 74, 59, 139

errors: as adults we make 104; how children correct errors 16; mathematical errors and utterances 15

even and odd numbers 101

expectations 59, 76, 125

explicit: explain thinking 79, 137; mathematical ideas in play 33, 34, 36, 37; mathematical intention 66, 69, 77, 102, 103, 128, 131, 142; making of unintentional ideas 141; possibilities in story 51, 52; use of puppets and props 4,98, 100, 105, 108, 111, 134, 140

extending ideas 43

facilitate: creative mathematical dialogue 71, 75, 82, 143; children's mathematical engagement 139; mathematical thinking 2, 114, 140

factors 53; other factors 75

Fairclough, R. 13

fish patterns 114

Fisher, R. 70, 72, 73, 75, 76, 82, 85, 88, 89, 93, 96, 142

flexibility: of oral storytelling 30, 89, 143; and engagement 47; of mathematical thinking 56; thinking 89

'Floss' 37

fluency 12, 17, 42, 144

Forest, H. 73

freedom 86; to follow ideas 12; a freer and more relaxed storyteller 86; free from text 30; freer with small groups 75, 89; freer with thinking 142

Freya retells 'Penguin' with precision and imagination 116

Frobisher et al 14, 15

Frobisher, L. 79, 101

Gallas, K. 74

games 54

generalisations: imaginitive 79; mathematical 5, 12, 14, 19, 71, 82, 88, 134; observation tool 17, 42; and pattern 13, 14, 15, 28, 81, 91, 135, 136, 137, 142; of story 1

genuine participation 70, 75, 76, 86

Ginnis, S. and Ginnis, P. 35, 37

'Goldilocks and the Three Bears' 9, 26, 48

'Goodnight Gorilla' 103, 110

group size 75, 85

Grugeon, E. and Gardner, P. 2, 4, 29, 30
guage: children's participation 75; with smaller groups 82
guided participation 32

hand puppet 4, 99, 103, 104, 105, 109, 110, 141, 154
'Handa's Return Journey' 95, 100, 120, 132
'Handa's Surprise' 20, 21, 22, 27, 31, 95, 100, 120, 132, 148
Hartman, B. 74, 95, 129, 130, 136
Haylock, D. 12, 82
Haylock, D. and Cockburn, A. 7, 11, 13, 14, 15, 28, 38, 53, 62, 79, 80, 81, 90, 91, 92, 113, 119, 133, 134, 135, 142, 143, 150
Haynes, J. and Murris, K. 4, 45, 76, 82, 87, 96, 133
height of wall 60, 123, 153
Hersh, R. 1, 5, 10, 11
Hong, H. 46, 48, 50, 51, 56, 76
hook: and attention 27, 32, 60; hooks 62; hooked 63, 64; repetitive phrases 95, 130
how to make a gorilla handpuppet 154–156
Hughes, M. 54, 100, 131, 142
'Humpty Dumpty' 30, 57, 58, 59, 60, 61, 62, 63, 64, 68, 77, 152, 153
Hutchins, P. 3, 22, 45, 47, 51, 54, 150

illustrations 6, 55, 60, 62, 149, 150, 153
imagination: and emotions 1; is a neglected tool of learning 30; one person's 25; oral storytelling stokes the 128; puppets and props capture the 99, 100; retelling mathematical story with precision and 112–13, 116, 125; as successful quality of children's stories 26; transforming mathematics with 32
Imai, M. 58, 63, 66, 69, 107, 152
implicit: implicitly and explicitly mathematical 3; play as implicitly mathematical 33, 34, 36, 37, 44; mathematics in puppet and prop making 111; mathematical ideas in story 128
interactive white board 84
internalise: ideas by children 82, 118, 119; mathematical ideas 71–2; story maps as a tool to 65
isomorphism 12, 15

'Jack and the Bean Stalk' 105
Jake 18, 38, 39, 40, 41, 42, 43, 44, 50, 118, 140

kaleidoscopic 35, 44
Keat, J.B. and Wilburne, J.M. 47, 48, 99
Kelham, S. 49, 74, 75, 85, 86, 90, 93, 112, 128, 140
key ideas 140
key word 65
'Knock, Knock, Teremok!' 128
Koshy, V. 12
Kuyvenhoven, J. 127, 128, 130

'Ladybird on a Leaf': a boy listens to 34, 39; a child retelling 16, 18, 38, 94, 119; clipboard drawing 78; a completed observational tool 42–3; mathematical map 133; mathematical pattern 79, 100, 135; playing with story-related props 40, 41, 44, 50, 105, 106
language of comparison 80
language: of addition 90; children use language of story 14, 71, 79; of comparison 80; to make mathematical ideas explicit 66; story language 53; of story supports mathematical language 51
large and small groups: reflections on telling stories to 84; video recorded working with 127
large groups: challenges of telling oral story to 3, 74, 75; children as peripheral participants 76; discussions 73; experience with 71, 84–5, 143; and genuine participation 82, 86; quieter children 94; storyteller perspective 77
Lave, J. and Wenger, E. 75, 76, 82, 116, 139
learning characteristics 56; see also learning-supportive characteristics
learning stories 2, 12, 17
learning-supportive characteristics 45, 54, 56, 61, 141, 142
Lewis, K. 37
Lipke, B. 130
Lipman, D. 95, 130
listener 97, 105, 113
'Little Lumpty' 105, 106, 107
Little Lumpty character: autistic child 68; character in picture book 30; explicit mathematical idea 66–7, 69; learning-supportive characteristics 61–6; and relationship between story and maths 57, 59, 60, 62, 68, 77; retelling with mathematical intention 63, 65, 122; story language 95; story prop 58, 99, 105, 106, 107, 125
Lord, J.V. and Burroway, J. 22, 47
lower ability 66, 67, 69, 94, 140; see also ability

magic: of the story 65; pot 74, 76; magical powers to double 105; magical pond 112–13, 117

making mathematical ideas explicit 100, 142; see also explicit

managing props and story 134

managing story and mathematical relationships 134

manipulating numbers 18, 62

map: of mathematical ideas 3; and observation 16, 41; story 65, 113, 142; mathematical 132, 133, 142

Mason, J. 133, 142

matching 15, 37, 101, 110

mathematical behaviour: capture with observational tool 3, 5, 7, 12, 16, 17, 34, 41, 141, 142; captures Jake's 41; talk unifies 72; and close connection with children's 84; see also behaviour; see also small groups

mathematical beings: storytellers as 142; tuning into our 142

mathematical errors 15–16; see also errors

mathematical experience 16, 50, 67, 85, 93, 134, 139; see also creative

mathematical facts 17, 42, 134, 144

mathematical idea: abstraction of 80; accessing 94, 96; context of story to explain 14, 29, 32, 47, 48, 54, 56, 69, 82, 137; connection between 53; of counting in multiples 65, 68, 107; challenge to communicate 74; connecting story with 77, 90, 113, 120, 124, 142; concrete representation of 106; of generalising and abstracting 71; in 'Goodnight Gorilla' 103; imagine 105; Jake works through 40; and 'Little Lumpty' 59; making explicit 66, 98–100, 131; pattern 79, 115; in play 34; playing with plot to prompt 11, 52, 132, 143; props support construct of 118; pursue more challenging 50; relationship between story and 48, 60–3, 135; in 'The Elves and the Shoemaker' 102

mathematical intention 7, 38, 63, 66, 69, 94, 107, 131, 137, 142

mathematical language: high profile of 94; insight into children's 142; oral story promotes 32; of ordinality 104; perceptive description using 67; positional language 60; practice using 51

mathematical learning 46, 48, 51, 54,56, 66; see also supportive learning characteristics

mathematical lens 3, 16, 34

mathematical maps 132, 133; see also maps

mathematical narrative: children as authors in play 3, 15, 24, 33, 36, 38, 44; definition of 24, 32; and oral 41, 128; as mode of knowledge 32

mathematical observation; see observation

mathematical possibilities 1, 3, 13, 46, 51, 53, 59, 64, 89, 125, 132, 147, 149, 151, 153

'Mathematical Storyteller Kings and Queens' 118

mathematical thinking: challenges of facilitating 4; children challenging their own 125; creative 108; disrupts children's 82; engage in 2; flexibility of 56; implicit in play 36; playing with plot to prompt 9, 24; picture books and 47–8, 51; and prop and puppet making 111

mathematical understanding 7, 9, 28, 34, 81, 113, 132

mathematical utterances 16, 17, 42, 47, 144

mathematicians 15, 79

mathematics in making props or puppets 109

Matterson, E. 57

McGrath, C. 10, 11, 22, 36, 67, 68, 76, 79, 101, 102, 104, 108, 110, 118, 119, 120, 130, 135

McQuillan, M. 22, 23, 24, 25

memory 24, 50, 72, 104, 130

Mercer, N. 72–73

Merttens, R. 101

modelling dialogic habits 89

moments of connection 129, 140, 142

motivation: mathematical 48, 66; and oral story 75; and puppet characters 99, 106, 110; and successful learners 47

multiples of 15; see also counting

multiplication: and algorithm 12, 17, 42; language and area of wall 61; and a network of connections 65; and repeated addition 64

'My Cat Likes to Hide in Boxes' 48, 49, 84

Naik, M. 74, 89

narrative 16, 17, 20, 22, 23, 24, 25, 28, 36, 41, 50, 72, 75

narrative: children as mathematical narrative authors 36; description of children retelling a story 16, 72; and observational tool 17, 41, 42; stories are not just 28; supports memory 50; of teaching 75; understanding of 20, 22, 23, 24, 25

narratology 23

nervousness 75; nervous 105, 119

'Never Give In' 126

'No Problem!' 5, 6, 7, 16, 27, 46, 53
nourish 71, 72, 73, 97, 99, 110
number bonds 15, 115
number combination tasks 50
number complement: Freya extends a story to try 116, 118, 120, 121, 140; and flexible storytelling 143; Jake creates his own 50; as part of an interactive story 114, 116, 118, 120, 121, 140, 143
number of people 59, 60, 153
number operations 53
number pattern 34, 62, 65, 89, 94, 140, 149, 151, 153
number relationships 15; children structuring 140; Freya works through 118; Jake talks through 41, 44; and 'Little Lumpty' 61–2; puppets and props 106; and 'The Door Bell Rang' 51–2, 55, 56
number stories 47
numerator 53
Numicon 37

observation: format 2, 16; framework i; of Jake 38, 42–3, 50; observations 12, 13; outcome of discussion with child and parent 17, 43; of play 44; record 142; tool 3, 5, 7, 12, 15, 16, 17, 34, 41, 141, 142, 144; see also small groups
observation: outcome of discussion with child and parent 17, 43
odd and even numbers 94, 98, 101, 102
'One City, Two Brothers' 77
one less than 22, 149
one to one correspondence 15; and counting accurately with 121
oral mathematical narrative 24, 32, 41
oral mathematical stories: build with children 88; crafting of 128; definition of 24; encourage children and adults to work with 2, 23; Freya retelling 4; as a pedagogical approach 4, 59, 81; from picture books to 57; possibilities of 82; promote mathematical language 32; props and puppets 111; retelling of 3; small group work 89; taking to children 108;
oral mathematical story teller: novice 105, 110; children as 4, 31; challenging for children 119, 139–40, 143
ordering 48, 50, 104
ordinal: value 99; language 103; ordinality 99, 104
Oxford Dictionary 98

Paley,V. 41, 142
parents 2, 16, 41, 74, 142
Parkinson, R. 89, 129, 142
participation 71: guided 32; opportunities for 54, 55, 62; genuine 70, 76, 82, 86; gauging 74, 75; legitimate peripheral 82
pattern: of addition 91; articulation of 14, 15, 18, 67, 73, 77, 95, 135; of bricks in wall 64; a child's own choice of 34; children sense a mathematical 8, 28, 134, 142; that can be generalised 17, 42, 79, 137; identifying characteristics of 2; Jake creates 40; and 'Ladybird on a Leaf' 100, 106, 136, 140; mathematical idea connects to 82; number 62, 65, 66, 84, 89, 99; questions to prompt generalising about 13, 80; recognising 11; of story 3, 13, 23, 56, 61, 121, 125, 128, 132, 134; and 'The Door Bell Rang' 53
pedagogical: alternative approach 4, 51, 69, 86, 96, 139, 143; literature as a choice 3, 45, 46; story as a tool 2, 20, 22, 28, 32, 56, 59, 81
'Penguin': alongside children 143; children as tellers of 116–118; 120–122, 125, 139; retold by Suzanne 112–114, 128; and pattern of fish 115; 128, and where told 130;
Piaget, J. 54
picture books: analysis of 2; engage children 3; evoke mathematical thinking 51; of high quality 141; mathematical opportunities in 4, 22; meaningful mathematical contexts 45–8, 56; moving to oral story 57–69; number stories in 47; and relationship between story and maths 51
Play for Tomorrow 35, 44
play: audio recordings of 7, 16; children as mathematical authors in 33, 36, 38, 44; dictaphone to record 23; difficult to define 23; Jake's 38, 40, 41, 43; mathematics and 3, 7, 15, 44, 72, 79; mathematical behaviour in 3, 5, 7, 12, 17, 41, 42, 43, 142; narratives 10, 44, 72; with plot 1, 3, 10, 24, 29, 47, 52, 53, 77, 89, 113, 143; with story related materials 12, 15, 16, 19, 34, 43, 48, 55, 81, 100, 118, 139; and story retellings 4; and threading in a mathematical way 33–44; through a mathematical lens 3, 34, 44; and tip of thinking 35; and transfer of mathematical ideas to 17, 42–3;uncertainty of 11, 41, 44; see also Hong; see also creative mathematical dialogue; see also smaller groups; see also mathematical

observation tool; *see also* children playing with story as storytellers; *see also* possibility thinking; *see also* pedagogical approach
plight 25, 27
Polya, G. 9, 11
polydron; and creating a net 49
pose and solve problems 3, 34, 41, 44; *see also* problem posing and solving
positional language 37, 44, 60, 119, 128, 149
possibility thinking 92; through creative dialogue 83, 89; and creative mathematical thinking 108; framed by what if? 13; of play 35; and prompts 89, 90, 96
Pound, L. 36, 49
Pound, L. and Lee.T. 2, 4, 13, 34, 44, 72, 73, 124, 127, 140
power 1, 30, 32, 47, 51, 75, 128; powerful 14, 30, 96, 143; overpower 46, 134; magical powers 105
Pratt, N. 32
predictional 14; predict 15, 79; predictable 96; unpredictable 36, 41, 44, 74; unpredictability 74, 95
prime number 12
principle of pairing 98, 101, 102
problem creating 9, 141
problem posing 3, 9, 10, 11, 17, 22, 36, 42, 108, 141
problem posing and problem solving 3, 5, 7, 8, 10, 13, 16, 18, 34, 36, 44, 61, 110, 140
problem solver 7, 9, 11
problem solving 3, 7, 9, 11, 13, 16, 22, 29, 36, 46, 72, 108, 110, 111, 141
prompt mathematical ideas 47, 52, 132
prompt mathematical thinking 3, 24, 96, 123; *see also* possibility thinking
proof 12, 14
prop making guide 109; *see also* puppets and props
properties of shapes 73; *see also* shapes
props and puppets 4, 99, 110, 111, 139, 140, 141; *see also* puppets and props
puppets and props: 4; and mathematical stories 97–113; *see also* props and puppets
purposeful 4, 16, 44, 91–2, 97, 99, 105, 111

qualities of stories 20, 22, 26
questions: drive mathematics 10, 11; and Egan 30; and future 143; and Hughes 100; and 'Ladybird' 39; and picture books 46; to prompt mathematical generalising 15, 80;

response to 40; skilful 90, 96; story related 24, 27; what if? 13, 53
quieter children 93, 94

Ransome, A. 33, 34, 119, 128
Rathmann, P. 103, 109, 110
Rayner, C. 1, 105
reasoning 13, 15, 16, 37, 134
recall 15, 65, 103, 104, 108, 110, 121; *see also* memory
receptive language 68
recording: 4, 7, 16, 41, 43, 65, 117, 142; of children 119, 142; data 11; DVD of Jake 43; of general statements about number 14; and making props and puppet 111; and reflecting 15; sharing with parents 43; systematic 92; of a television documentary 35; value of 41; 41, 86
rectangle 73; *see also* shape
reflecting 15, 37, 129
relationship: and children connect to new mathematical 139; between children, stories and tellers 97, 99, 110; between even and odd 102; and groups of children 75; and inviting ideas 89; and 'Lumpty's Ladder' 62, 65; managing story and mathematical 134–36; between narrative and story 24; and number 15, 41, 43–4, 50–3, 55–6, 62, 106, 115, 118, 135, 140; between storyteller, prop and story 110; between storyteller and mathematical ideas 137, 142; between story and audience 30; between story, maths and play 143; between story and maths 4, 8, 10, 16, 19, 22, 32, 45, 51, 56–7, 60, 69, 89, 132, 134; between problem posing and solving 10, 18, 36; between story read and story told 3; unintentional 141; between using words and understanding ideas 32; to work with 3; *see also* learning-supportive characteristics
repetitive: and phrase 27, 32, 60, 84, 95, 96, 102, 119, 130; and EAL children 96
representation: algebraic 14; hand puppet 110; for recall 14, 65; physical 140; prop or puppet as concrete representation of 99, 106, 108; of story characters 99; symbolic 105; *see also* abstract
resolution 136
rhythm; of stories 31
risk 11, 59, 65, 69, 74, 136
ritual 88, 139
road map for mathematics 132

Rogoff, B. 29
Russian tale 33, 34, 119, 127, 128

scaffold 32, 105, 111, 141; and removing of 105–6
Schiro, M. 4, 29, 30, 32, 46, 140, 142
scope 54, 55, 61, 71
sequence 14, 15, 22, 23, 24, 26, 27, 32, 52, 65, 66; and sequential 8, 22
Shakespeare, W. 112
Shapes: 2D 73, 74, 88; 3D 73, 74, 88; circle 73, 88, 89, 96, 104, 124; cube 88; cuboid 88; diamond 88; hexagon 83, 88, 124, 128; oval 73; pentagon 83, 88,124, 128; septagon 124; square 83, 88, 96, 124, 128
size 60
small group oral mathematical storytelling: 'Blue Egg Dinosaur' story 90; how children respond 4, 83, 93–4, 96; and creative mathematical dialogue 82; a different learning experience 88; more intimate quality 96; 'Little Lumpty' 131; opening out 85, 89; 'Penguin' 113; see also large groups; see also large and small groups
sociocultural theory 29
Stanford, P. 89, 143
starting sentence 130; see also hook
'Stone Soup' 73
story language 16, 19, 41, 43, 53, 79, 94, 142; see also language
story listener 87, 88, 96, 122
story map 65, 113, 130, 140
story profile 2, 3, 27, 56, 60, 141, 142; template 146; 'The Doorbell Rang' by Pat Hutchins 150; 'Handa's Surprise' by Eileen Browne 148; 'Little Lumpty' by Miko Imai 152
story structure 20, 26, 27, 32, 47, 120, 139
story-related materials 12, 38, 48, 140: see also props and puppets
storyteller: ability of 79, 89; can articulate generalisations 79; children as 3, 10, 12, 71, 72, 88, 112–125, 139, 143; confidence as 86, 111; crafting and telling 129; educators as 84, 96; extracts of conversation with children 92; and flexibility 89; free from text 30; as mathematical beings 133; perspective 77; professional 2, 37, 71, 77, 111, 127, 128, 129; secure mathematical vocabulary 32; challenge of 56, 74, 134, 139; see also making mathematics explicit; see also small group work; see also creative mathematical

dialogue; see also relationships; see also props and puppets; see also Vygotsky
strategies: contextualise 16; connections among 16; counting 104; lining Ladybird spots up 16; mental 18, 62; problem solving 7, 11, 16, 46; see also checking; see also one to one correspondence
subtraction: and addition connections 124; algorithm 12; building on patterns 14; for comparison 80; complements 15, 100, 106; and 'Handa's Surprise' 149; Jake works out number relationships using 41; and 'Ladybird' story 135; and mathematical maps 132; and story 120; and 'The Doorbell Rang' 151
Suggate et al. 7, 73, 82, 113, 132, 137
supportive learning characteristics 2, 3, 46, 54
surprise: children classed as lower ability 66, 67; child with autistic characteristics 66; children acquiring English 66; class teacher is surprised 59; and disrupt mathematical thinking 82; at how skilled children are 139; Mya surprises me 131; oral mathematical story bring 82; oral mathematical story offers possibility of 140; surprises 65; trainee educators are surprised 47, 66, 67
symbol: of addition 90; symbolising (using symbols) 15; symbolic learning 30; symbolic representation 105
symmetry 1, 2
systematic: chidren encouraged to be 92; follows instructions 16; recording 92; strategy for problem solving 7; ways of setting out information 8; working 15; see also strategies

Talk for writing 65
'Teremok' 33, 34, 37, 38, 44, 119, 121, 127, 128
The Book of Lieh-Tzu: A classic of Tao 126
'The Doorbell Rang' 3, 22, 39, 45, 47, 50, 51, 53, 54, 56
'The Elves and the Shoemaker' 4, 79, 94, 97, 98, 101, 102, 108
'The Enormous Turnip' 77, 81, 128, 129
'The Giant Jam Sandwich' 22, 47
'The Greedy Triangle' 47, 83, 84, 85, 86, 88, 123, 124, 128
'The Man Who Moved a Mountain' 126
'The Old Woman and her Pig' 26
'The Tempest' 112
'The Three Little Pigs' 26
thinking string 66, 67, 69, 131

three number components 50
tiger 1, 2, 105, 11, 143
Toy Hong, L. 70, 74, 76, 94, 105
Trevarthen, C. 35
trial and error 7, 110, 111, 143
triangle 83, 84, 88, 96, 124, 128; *see also* shape
'Two of Everything' 70, 74, 76, 94, 105

unpredictability 74; *see also* predictional

Van den Heuvel-Panhuizan, M. and Elia, I. 3, 46, 54, 56, 60, 141
Van den Heuvel-Panhuizan, M. and Van den Boogaard, S. 46, 47, 48, 51, 56
Vera John-Steiner and Ellen Souberman 72
Vijfde zijn ('Being Fifth') 47
visualisation of mathematical ideas 100, 111, 141
visualiser 84
vocabulary: of mathematics 32; of story 50; *see also* language
Vygotsky, L. 29, 33, 35, 44, 51, 71, 72, 82, 119, 125, 141, 142

Walker, B. 127
Walshe, L. 66
Walter, M. 11
Weaver, S. 47
Welchman - Tishler, R. 46
what if?: asking 10, 36, 141–42; conjectural question 13, 17, 35, 140, 144; at the heart of problem solving 13; learning disposition 12–13; opens out new problems 141; poses a new problem 8; possibility thinking 13, 35, 41, 53, 147, 149, 151, 153; question playing with plot 24; reshaping story 143
'Who Lived in the Skull?' 34, 128
whole class 16, 84, 85, 86, 89, 93, 94, 96, 116, 140
Wye, C. 105, 111, 126, 127, 128, 129

Yeats, W.B. 83, 97

Zebra skin 2
Zone of Proximal Development 29; *see also* Vygotsky
Zoomy numbers 123; *see also* counting in multiples